MW01294503

Marn

Kim Harris Stowell

Copyright © 2020 Kim Harris Stowell

All rights reserved.

ISBN: 9781793456540

DEDICATION

To my beloved family

INTRODUCTION

Marnie was my grandmother. A remarkable woman, she was a tremendous force in my life, and in the lives of so many others. I think of her as the Kunta Kinte of our family; children are told the story of her life and times, and her legacy lives on in all of us.

As her eldest grandchild, I am fortunate to have gotten so much of her. Some of my earliest memories are of visiting her on a farm where she rented a little two-bedroom apartment for many years. I remember how she could not contain her excitement as my little brother and I ran up the lawn toward her hug; she fairly trembled with anticipation. The big toy chest always stood behind the wing chair in her living room, filled with a modest assortment of old-fashioned and timeworn toys, and we loved finding them all there each time we went to see her. We were so sure of her from the very start.

Marnie and her grandchildren Kim and Stephen

When her oldest daughter – my mother – died suddenly and

young, Marn took my siblings and me in, at a time when three young grandchildren were the last things she needed underfoot. She was more or less a newlywed at the time, and was enjoying, for the first time in a very long time, the feeling of being cared for. Responsibility had finally been lifted off her shoulders. And then we came along. But she – and her husband – took us in gladly, and I have said more than once that the year I spent living with her was – ironically, considering my mother had just died – one of the best years of my life. She taught me so many important lessons during that time, some of which I did not understand for years to come.

Let me say at this point that Marn was no angel, at least not in the generally accepted understanding of the word. If you're okay with the image of an angel with a bourbon in one hand and a cigarette in the other, who may have slept with someone else's husband once or twice, and could possibly have lied to a bill collector or two over the years, then maybe we can work something out.

So yes, we're talking a different kind of angel, one that often wears those tiny little red or powder blue Keds, and maybe has a bit of lipstick on one of her big front teeth, but has a Boston accent as heavy as any Red Sox announcer and stories that will have you roaring with laughter. And in the summer, throw on the sunburn that we have all come to know as the Marnie Nose, the result of many a sunny day spent outdoors – by a pool, at the

beach or on a boat -- with her omnipresent big dark sunglasses on. When you get right down to it, Marn was at the same time larger than life and unabashedly human, a neat trick if you can do it.

I felt her strong presence during my teen and college years, as she made special efforts to keep our connection alive in some very powerful ways, despite my great existential ennui. And later, when my first child was born, we made such a joyous circle. Marnie's health was failing then, and she was somewhat fuzzy when it came to short-term memory. For her, sitting on the sofa with a baby was a perfect pastime and an absolute delight. The two of them would grin at each other, making little noises and giggling. And in a thin little voice, weakened by medical treatments and lack of breath, Marnie sang the songs to my Sarah that she had sung when I was a tot. For me, sitting across the room with the crossword puzzle and a cup of coffee, it was the show of a lifetime.

When Marn died, I felt the earth shift under my feet, so strong was the loss of her for me. I was in my late twenties and a young mother, and when I heard the news, I went out into our front yard and stared at the sky for a long time. I called to her, whispering her name over and over. "Don't go," I cried, "I need you!" I was overcome with a sense of stark, utter loneliness. I walked away down our dirt road, trudging along as if on a treadmill, while I struggled to find my emotional equilibrium. When I finally got back home, my dad called, and I found I couldn't speak a word to him through the new round of sobs his call launched.

Through the entire memorial service in celebration of Marnie's life, I wept uncontrollably, to the point where well-meaning relatives turned around in their pews and gave me sad looks. I can't tell you anything about that service. I loved her so.

Later that night, when we all sat in her living room on Old Sudbury Road, I dared to wonder out loud how we would keep our family together. Marnie had been the matriarch -- all the holiday celebrations were held at her house, news of us all traveled through her -- she was our rock.

That moment was the beginning of 20 wonderful summers of annual get-togethers, called Family Frolics, held in her memory at the big, welcoming home of her youngest daughter Polly. We came from far and wide, bringing tents, coolers, babies, dogs, swimsuits and tennis racquets, and generally celebrated our love for each other in a three-day blowout party.

We always told the Marnie stories. We sang the Marnie songs. I think we were all in agreement that Marn had taught us everything we knew about love and family and fun, and we honored her in that way every year. We became convinced that she controlled the weather, as we so rarely had anything but sunny, mild weather for those late June weekends. We don't have frolics anymore, but we have cemented relationships as a result of them so that I'm sure we will never drift apart.

But back to Marn. I set out on this venture to try and write what it was that made her so extraordinary. This turned out to be much harder than I thought it would be. I asked my cousin Chip to describe what it was that made her special, and he said, "It was all in her facial expressions." Fabulous. Many others came up empty too, unable to put into words what it was about her. Don't worry though – a sufficient number of stories were told and retold to make for one hell of a portrait of this amazing lady.

Marn had a tough life, as you'll soon agree. A rocky childhood, divorce and single motherhood at a young age, the woes of poverty, and troubles of most every kind came her way at some point. But while there are surely other people who had it even worse, I daresay not many of them ever took things in stride the way my grandmother Marnie did. There really was just something about her – her ability to laugh and cry at the same time, her courage to go out and get a job and  raise her three daughters by herself, at a time when single mothers were entirely uncommon, and her wisdom and sense of fun. Especially her sense of fun. Marnie had an indomitable spirit, and those of us who were lucky enough to be touched by it will never be the same.

Kim Harris Stowell

Upper Brookville, New York, Summer 2011

PART ONE

She wasn't always called Marnie – that came when she had grandchildren, although I'm not sure how. I always thought I made it up, but other family members say she chose it. You may choose to believe either version, as will I. Before she was Marnie, she was Midge to most people. But for the record, she was born Marjorie Katherine Vahey, in Watertown, Massachusetts in July of 1911, the daughter of Eleanor and Martin Vahey, both grandchildren of

proud Irish immigrants. Marn had two older sisters, Eleanor and Mary, and a younger brother named Jack. It was a happy family, and our hero enjoyed a special place in the

Martin and Eleanor Vahey

hearts of her parents, whom she adored. She was (according to her) the apple of her father's eye. But if you asked her, she was the apple of virtually

7

everyone's eye.

The early photographs portray a robust American family living a comfortable life for the early 1900s. They had a nice home in town, with a housekeeper named Prudence and a cook named Mrs. Lavely. The four Vahey children were off to a good start and seemed destined for a comfortable future. Sadly, though, things would not always be so idyllic, as this happy home was headed for a very tragic turn, the first of many for Midge Vahey.

After a brief but turbulent illness, my great grandmother Eleanor Louise Morris Vahey succumbed to a great flu epidemic, dying along with so many others in 1918. Little Marjorie was but seven years old.

She had also been very sick — it was in fact the child whom everyone thought would not survive the terrible virus. Feverish and listless, the little girl drifted in and out of a tumultuous sleep for days, tended to by Prudence and a nurse from town, since her mother was also ailing and had not the strength to care for her. But in the course of one night, after a week of much bedside concern and hand-wringing, the child began to show signs of improvement. To everyone's great relief, she was able to sip some tea and sit up in her bed. At the same time, however, her mother's health was declining rapidly.

The next morning, Mrs. Lavely brought young Marjorie a bowl of thin oatmeal, which she finished. She got up, feeling shaky and weak, but quite a lot better. Prudence asked if she might like to visit with her mother, to which she said yes and was led to the bedroom door. Inside, all the shades were drawn and the air was thick and still, giving the room a heavy, foreboding feel. She shuffled quietly into Ella's bedroom, while Prudence waited in the doorway.

As Marn stood by her mother's bedside, the morbidly ill woman opened her tired eyes and, reaching out a weakened hand, stroked her daughter's cheek. "Midgie," she said in a reedy voice, "Oh, my Midgie. They'll cut your hair."

She was to die shortly thereafter.

And so the Vahey children were left without a mother. Eleanor, the oldest, was almost twelve, and baby Jack was five. So grief-stricken was their father that he shut himself in his office at the back of the house, refusing to take meals or sleep. Prudence and Mrs. Lavely cared for the children through the days that followed, and dressed them that Saturday for the church service in memory of their mother. The family walked the sad distance to the church, scarcely noticing their surroundings, and their father Martin broke down in sobs as he stood at the lectern, thanking all the well-wishers who had come to pay their respects. It was a heartbreaking loss.

The children were moved almost immediately following their mother's funeral into the home of their maiden aunts Mary and Rose, sisters of their father. They stood in shock as their belongings were packed into trunks and boxes and they were dressed in their finest outfits to go and stay with two ladies they hardly knew.

Their father lived there too at first, but he was not around much. So traumatized was he by the loss of his wife that seeing the children made his heart break all over again. So he took a house in the next town and left the care of the children to his sisters. He was never out of their lives completely, but the children are said to have been raised by the aunts.

As her dying mother had predicted, little Midgie's hair was indeed cut, and the life to which she and her siblings were accustomed ended abruptly as they entered a very different world. Their pets, a cat named Strawberry Jam and a young collie named Pete, were given to a farm outside of town, and they scarcely had time to say goodbye to their neighbors and their familiar surroundings before they found themselves in a dark old house on the noisy main road through town. But as if those circumstances weren't bad enough, the fact was that Aunt Mary

The children plus a couple of extras.

and Aunt Rose were drunks, plain and simple. Both approaching spinster age, they were raging alcoholics. They were both oddities too: Aunt Mary was very mousy and quiet — a little spooky — and she was forever taking a backseat to her sister. Aunt Rose, on the other hand, was a formidable woman, big and beefy.

The two of them had just enough on the ball to keep up appearances, but neither had much interest in the children's welfare beyond enjoying their company, but this they did immensely. They were seriously neglectful when it came to basic needs, but they clearly loved the children very much — "Even," as Marn would say, "Sissy," referring to Mary, the second oldest child. Sissy was a difficult child, rigid and prone to jealousy. She was probably jealous of Marn, who always had such a goddamned sunny outlook. I'd say Sissy had the misfortune to be the middle child, with all the psychological challenges that come with that, but she was apparently pretty unpleasant all her life. The stories do not reflect very well on her.

On the other hand, the eldest child, Eleanor, was charming. Known all her life as Nana, she had a big personality with a boisterous style and a quick grin. She was precocious as a girl, delighting all her younger siblings with her clowning ways and physical antics when they were babies and toddlers.

The aunts and the children

But everything changed for Nana when her mother died.

Being the oldest, she had no one looking out for her, sticking up for her or paving the way for her. She felt a little unsafe in the world.

And after a few years of living with the two boozy aunts as her guardians, Nana began to venture out of familiar territory, sneaking away from the house when she could get out from under all her siblings. She became a bit of a wild thing, as Marn would say, living the high life in her teens and getting into trouble, about which Aunt Mary and Aunt Rose were completely unaware. Even when a teacher called at the house one evening to report that Nana had gotten into some sort of trouble, they took no apparent notice.

Just getting an unexpected evening visitor was unusual enough, and when the doorbell rang that night, all the children were fairly certain it had something to do with Nana, who was noticeably absent. They hid behind the long draperies in the parlor as Aunt Rose walked the long hallway from the kitchen to answer the front door. Sure enough, it was Nana's teacher. The woman was not asked in, and although the children strained their little ears to hear what was transpiring, they heard nothing. When she said her goodbye, Aunt Rose came in from the porch, turned and went back to the kitchen, with the kids creeping along stealthily behind her. With their ears to the door they heard her mutter, "Well, it seems one of the children has gotten into trouble," to which Aunt Mary said, "Oh, is that it then?" And that was it. That was the end of it. There was no mention of it ever again. It was as though, in Aunt Rose's mind, the teacher had merely come by to impart some news.

So Nana was never reined in, and continued to run with her fast crowd. In today's world, we have explanations for why kids do stuff like that too – As the eldest, she was rebelling against a cruel world and her tough lot in it. The trouble kids can get into has changed since those days, but back then she was left mostly to her own devices, and was in many ways a tragic figure.

The youngest one, Jack, was Marn's favorite. A handsome, gentle child, she worshipped him, taking care of him like a mother even though she was only two years older than he. Jack tended to the quiet side, and was always very skinny. He had a talent for seeming

Jack Vahey.

invisible as a child. Each one of them had their way of dealing with living with the aunts, and his was to vanish while in plain sight. Marn used to say you couldn't see him at all if he turned to the side. There is a story that West Point Academy rejected his application because he was too thin, telling him to eat bananas, which he did and was eventually accepted.

One can only imagine what life was like at that house. The faces of the children in the few photos tell a story of a grim existence — no one is smiling. Their expressions are hard-set and resigned, almost as though they were still in shock. With no parenting and almost no caretaking at all, it was probably sometimes harrowing, especially for the older ones. Their old housekeeper Prudence sometimes stopped in – she had a new job with a new family, but she had grown to love the Vahey children. She would bring them bread and cakes when she could, and often tidied up the house when the aunts were not around. Prudence had a big heart and could see that the children were needy, but she simply had not the wherewithal to do much about it.

The four of them did their best to look out for one another, but they were so completely unprepared for this turn of events that they never really quite pulled it off. This is when you start to see Marn's nature come through, as she seemed to survive the best of all of them. While Nana ran off with the neighborhood hooligans and Sissy became angry and pinched, Midge didn't seem so much the worse for wear, as she would put it. All her life, she had an uncanny knack for knowing her circumstances and making the best of them. She may in fact have invented happy-go-lucky. She made friends easily as a child and was adored (according to her) by everyone she met. And she had an uncanny ability to bring out the best in people, so maybe she did so for the hard-drinking aunts too.

The stories that have stood the test of time are few, and run to the cockeyed, like the one about Jack and the bananas, and the night Nana's teacher came to call, and this one: Marn had lobster as a child. Each person was to take his or her own lobster down to the water and rinse it before eating it. Midge, so the story goes, took hers to the water and it swam away. She never liked lobster after that.

Marnie did well enough in school, although she had to work at it. I cannot honestly say that she was a brilliant mind, but she figured out how to get through school if you weren't maybe so smart: She was often the teacher's pet — she understood right from wrong, and used her sense of humor and magnetism to persuade her schoolmates to go along with her.

Her best friend for much of her teen years was Rosie Madden, who had been Nana's friend originally despite being much younger than she. Rosie was a fun-loving kind of gal, but maybe not as wild as Nana was. After an incident where Nana tried to get her to commit some minor infraction or other, Rose began to gravitate away from Nana and her crowd, turning instead to Marn, who was more Rosie's type as well as being closer to her in age. For the young Midge, it was so wonderful to have a pal with whom to escape, even momentarily, that dreary place she called home. The two became fast friends — I think they had similar outlooks on life — and their friendship lasted all their lives. They sang together in the school glee club, swooned over handsome boys, and generally had a ball. During a rough patch later on in her life, Marn even moved in for a while with Rose, who had at that point married and had a child. Rosie is still alive as I write this, at a nursing home in full Alzheimer's, having outlived Marn by more than 25 years. One of Marnie's daughters goes to visit her sometimes.

Martin Vahey had never been a regular father to Midge, but he had never been far away either, so she did have a relationship with him. He was the kind of guy who would come by and hoist the girls on his shoulders and race around the garden while they shrieked in delight. He brought the children small gifts from time to time: a baseball mitt for Jack, a doll for one of the girls, a bracelet for another.

Someone else (like me for example) might say that this was just more neglect heaped on these poor children, but for Marn, it was enough. She was not a stickler for the formalities of relationships. She felt loved by him, and it was the love and the feelings that mattered. It is as though his affection sustained her, giving her what she needed as she grew into a young woman.

She played basketball in high school, and very well if you asked her. She also allowed as how she was very popular. We have no way to verify either of these claims, but I don't doubt the popularity one at all. People just seemed drawn to her all her life. Seemingly so unlikely – shabby-poor, and not a looker by any means with her buck teeth and unruly hair – she nevertheless commanded attention from those around her.

When she was a senior in high school, Midge had a solo in the spring production at school. She was so proud, as the part was greatly sought after, and she was not particularly known for being musical. But when she delivered her splendid rendition of whatever song it was, she surprised her entire class by knocking it right out of the old ballpark. The audience was floored! Later, the music teacher suggested she go to a radio station in Boston and apply for a job opening. The station manager was looking for someone to perform each week, right before the Dinah Shore program came on. Heralded in the family record of Big Accomplishments, Marn auditioned for and got the job. It was a fifteen-minute program, and she sang the standards of the day. Her voice was light and lilting, with a liveliness that came right from her personality.

The show was quite popular and, as she was just graduating from high school, she might have continued following that path, creating a career for herself – or at least getting her foot in the door somewhere. But she stopped singing when she married Ted Robinson, who did not approve of his wife having a career.

It would be more accurate to say Marn stopped singing professionally when she married Ted. She continued to sing, hum, whistle and harmonize almost non-stop for the rest of her life.

Midge met Ted Robinson at a military base social mixer, which she attended with her old pal Rosie Madden and Rosie's boyfriend Todd Kenney. An attractive man, Ted was making his career in the Air Force, and he swept her off her feet. She was crazy about him, crazy enough to wait for almost three years while he finished school before they got married. For Marnie, it was a fairy tale romance.

Once she married my grandfather, Midge gave birth to three daughters – Linda Martin, Susan Hamilton and Paulina Lane, known as Polly – in fairly rapid succession. There is barely two years between any of their birthdays, so she went from being a single gal to a mother of three in no time. But she thoroughly embraced it, along with her new role as military wife. It was a good life, and she enjoyed it enormously – there were many opportunities to make friends and she was popular at parties. People just got a kick out of our Midge.

Here's a good story: One day, she was upstairs stripping the sheets off the beds. As she flung them down the staircase – a moment too late to do anything about it – she saw her husband's commanding officer standing at the foot of the stairs. The sheets, naturally, wrapped right around his head.

She flew down the stairs behind the sheets, one hand in front of her like a football player and the other clutching her heart as she ran, calling out silly partial sentences, "Oh, my good– I am so terribly… Here, let me…" She reached the bottom of the stairs, grabbed the corner of a sheet and pulled. The officer began to spin around in the front hall like a while cotton tornado.

It was just then that Ted walked back in, carrying some papers. It took him a minute to figure out what had happened. He held his breath as his superior officer composed himself. The gentleman turned to address Midge, but before he could get a word out, he began to chuckle. Marn hurriedly gathered up the sheets. The officer began to roar, and Marn could hold back no longer. She burst out with a laugh too, and the two of them told Ted, between giggles, what had occurred. Ted was a little unsure how to react, but his superior clapped him on the back, saying, "You've got yourself one hell of a wife, there, you have!" Ted, finally able to exhale, thanked him – and apologized for good measure – and the man left the house with the papers, shaking his head and laughing as he went.

Ted Robinson with Polly and Susan

Another story begins with Marn coming up from the cellar one day to hear a caterwauling that could only be baby Polly, upstairs in her crib. Marn raced up the steps, imagining blood and bruises and broken limbs. Grasping the knob at the top of the banister, she spun down the little hallway toward Polly's door and grabbed the doorknob, which promptly pulled out of the door, leaving her on one side and the little banshee on the other. The screams were getting louder and, as she went downstairs to call her husband at the base, Marn muttered under her breath, wondering at Polly's ability to make such a racket.

Ted was not able to come to the phone, his secretary said.

"Well, tell him I need help!" she sputtered, "Polly's locked in her room and she's yelling something awful."

"Oh, my! Yes, Mrs. Robinson," said the voice on the other end, a secretary that Marn had never met, "I'll let him know right away."

Marn thanked her and hung up, calmer now. But as she stood there in her kitchen, trying to be patient, she was serenaded anew by the screaming Polly, who seemed to have gotten a fresh burst of energy.

"At least she's still conscious," she thought to herself, and her eyes fell on the screwdriver kept on the shelf near the phone. Seizing it, she hurried back up the stairs and, in a flash, had jimmied the door open with it.

There was Polly, her face a reddened, runny mess, and the cast on her leg, where she recently had surgery, lodged between the bars of the crib.

"Oh, you silly goose, now how did you get yourself stuck like this?" she chided the little girl, as she chuckled quietly to herself. Thankful that it was only this and not something much worse, she turned the cast and slid the leg free, gathering the little girl into her arms. Slowly Polly quieted down to a light whimper as Marn sang softly to her, bouncing her gently in hopes that the nap could be resumed. Back and forth, back and forth they walked, soothing each other. Marn moved over to the dormer window, leaning Polly slightly so she could see the dooryard and the other houses on their street. To her great surprise, she peered out to see all manner of army vehicles – big and small — pulling up to the curb in front of the house. Her husband seemed to have summoned every rescue vehicle on the base to aid her in her rescue of the fair Polly.

And so she did what any smart army wife would do: Putting Polly back in the crib, she stuck the little cast between the same slats again, and, shutting the knobless door, went downstairs to welcome the help.

Linda

Marn loved the early years of motherhood and family. She was out of that dreadful house of her childhood, had a man that she adored, and all the creature comforts. Her children were developing into little people – Linda was considered to be very smart for her age and rather serious, and Susan was sweet, docile and always agreeable. Polly was a scrappy one, and quite the sprite. The baby of the family, little Polly was a handful.

Marn's old pal Rosie, who had by this time married Todd Kenney, was a steadfast friend in Marn's early years as a mother. The three little Robinson girls adored the two of them and always looked forward to their visits. Everyone loved their friendliness and their high spirits. They loved music and fun, so they fit in with the group as if born to it. And they were very much in love, which showed especially whenever they danced together. They often joined Midge and Ted at parties and other events on the Air Force base.

Unfortunately, the military life was short-lived for our Midge. Just shy of six years into their marriage, Marn learned of her husband's unfaithfulness. It seems Ted had gotten someone pregnant while overseas, and wrote a letter home to tell his wife he was leaving her for this other woman.

This news came as a complete shock to Marn. She was very much in love with him – Todd Kenney always said that Ted was the love of Midge's life – and she was certainly not expecting anything like this. Her pride was terribly hurt, and the fact that he wrote it in a letter instead of coming home to break the news made it even worse.

While no one was privy to whatever ensued during the conversations that followed – or even what the divorce itself was like – we do know that she told Ted in no uncertain terms that their official story was to be that she was the one who left him, not the other way around. In classic Marnie style, she figured out her circumstances quickly and made the best deal she could — she knew life ahead was going to be tough enough without being a woman whose husband left her.

Rose and Todd were right there for Midge when she needed them, visiting often and getting her to smile, something she sorely needed. They would stay up late into the night, laughing and talking, reassuring her that there was still plenty to be happy about. And she could cry with them too, especially Todd. She always said that Todd was like

Rose Madden and Todd Kenney

a big brother to her; he could see how crushed she was, and how hurt. While she felt the need to be strong for the others, especially her daughters, he was very chivalrous with her, allowing her vulnerable side to come out and confess that she was sad and afraid. She needed the chance to fall apart a little, and he made a safe place for her to do that. What a good friend he was to her.

Midge had no choice at first but to move in with her sister Nana, who was also divorced, but with a big alimony and a house on Beacon Street in Watertown where she lived with her son Dick Phinney. Nana was still the life of the party and, at this point, a bit of a lush. But she was warm and loving with the girls and always tried to be on good behavior when they were around. As a result, the girls were all crazy about Nana, and Marn was grateful for the roof over their heads. There was not a lot of room, so Linda and Susan slept in the same bed with Marn, Polly still being crib-sized.

Susan, Linda, Polly

On the first night they were there, she gathered the three girls as she was about to put Polly to bed in her crib, patting the white bedspread so the two older girls hopped up obediently and sat beside their little sister. While stroking the hair of first one girl, then another, she asked them what they thought. All three girls jumped to say how nice the arrangements were, anxious to cheer their mother. Each child tried to out-do the others with their enthusiasm.

She smiled at her sweet little bugs and fought back sudden tears. Her life had changed drastically, and she knew it, but she still had her girls. She also knew that she would do whatever it took to provide a good life for them. She made each child promise that they would be on their best behavior. This was not their house, she told them, so they must be quiet as mice and as helpful as they could be.

Once the girls had sworn they would be angels — all except Polly, who was too small to really understand any of it (and might not have gone along with it anyway) – Marn gathered them up in their special group hug. The sweet smell of a baby, just out of the bath, wafted to her and she felt a weight coming off her shoulders. She sighed, gazing at the three little faces around her, and asked them which one wanted to be the first to kiss their mother.

And the four of them turned into a giggling, squealing bundle of love, the girls covering their mother's face with kisses, as Marn tried to shush them. When at last they had quieted, she put Polly in her crib, an hour later tucking the other two into her own bed, where she would join them soon thereafter, exhausted from the day.

So for a time they made a life there. Linda was enrolled in school and Susan and Polly traveled around the area by bus with Marn as she looked for work. It was more than a little inconvenient to have the girls along while filling out applications or meeting with potential bosses. Little Susan would sit reverently watching the secretaries as one would gaze at a movie starlet, but Polly was a squirmer. So it was slightly miserable at times, but Midge had no choice. She did not want to leave them in the care of either Nana or the girls' cousin Dick. Dick was three years older than Linda, and was not thrilled to have all these little girls underfoot. Especially Polly the troublemaker. She still had that cast on her foot, and was now using little crutches, which she hated. In a tantrum one day, she flung her crutches over her head across the room, where they crashed into Dick's record collection,

Linda and Dick Finney

breaking almost every one of them. Dick was furious. He would have strangled her, but he'd have had to get past Marn first. That night, as he was walking by the bathroom where Polly was being given her bath, he stuck his head around the corner, threatening to dunk her head three times and bring it up twice. The three little Robinson girls were aghast to hear something so menacing; they were not accustomed to being spoken to in such a way, and they were scandalized. Dick Phinney basically tormented the girls the whole time they lived there.

Nana's house was right across the street from Aunt Rose and Aunt Mary – who had cared for Marn when she was a child. The big dark house sat next door to what was now the Perkins School for the Blind.

By then the Aunts were getting on in years, and still drinking to beat the band. But they still adored children, so Marn would take the girls to spend the occasional afternoon visiting them, as her way of thanking them for their earlier kindness in raising her. She had an odd affiliation with the Aunts – as much as she could not produce any happy memories of her time spent under their care, they were nevertheless the ones who had provided a roof over her head all those years.

As for the girls, going for these visits was not their favorite thing to do. It was a loomingly huge old house, first of all, and perpetually in disarray. Not dirty so much, but just disorganized. Books sat in messy stacks on tables rather than in the many tall bookshelves. Newspapers were piled up everywhere too, usually opened to the crossword puzzle. The kitchen was kept reasonably clean, but there was never much food or cooking going on. And then there were the aunts themselves, creepy old things, and a little scary sitting in their dark creepy old house. The girls found them intimidating, particularly Rose, who was known for having said, "I've never been married nor nothin'," which the girls tried to figure out the meaning of for years. She would drink all day from a mug of something she kept on top of the highest kitchen cabinet. (She called it orange juice; it was vodka.)

Rose was also a germophobe. The girls gathered their courage one day to ask their mother why Aunt Rose was perpetually spitting into the air. "She's spitting out germs," they were told. Her fear extended beyond her own self to the girls whenever she was in charge of them. The Aunts took Susan and Polly out to lunch once, while Marn went to a job interview. Rose insisted they wear gloves when they left the house, even eating in the restaurant with their white gloves on, and they had to bathe and change clothes when they returned home. It was very nice to be taken out for a meal (and since it was lunch, there was a modicum of sobriety), but they were a little afraid of Aunt Rose.

Susan was the possible exception; she claimed to enjoy the visits to the Aunts. Sometimes, she snuck through the fence between their house and the school next door, in a rare show of spunk, to play with the blind children. And she talked Linda one day into going for a visit, on their own, to see the Aunts while their mother was out, again looking for work. This was quite an undertaking, as the street that separated the two houses was four lanes wide and very busy. And let's not forget that they were five and seven years old. Holding hands, the two youngsters scrambled across the busy street, had their little visit with the two old pickles, and managed to make it back again safely too an hour later. Unfortunately for them, though, they arrived home at the same time as their mother, who stood on the steps, hands on hips, glaring at them as they approached. Their pace slowed, knowing they had been caught for a most grievous crime. When they finally reached the front steps, Marn resisted her inclination to gather them into a hug, so great was her relief at their safety. Instead she made very sure they knew how cross she was with them. In fact, this seems to have been the only time Linda was ever spanked.

This was a very low time for Marn, as she and her sister Nana had never been particularly close, and she was living in someone else's house without her belongings and no idea how she was going to get out and no friends. Marn was accustomed to having a cadre of people around her. And she had begun getting used to having a loving husband too. So she felt more than a little off balance. And not knowing anyone made it hard to have fun, let alone manage in an emergency. Early in their time at Nana's the girls were playing out in the yard when Linda came in screaming for her mother. Polly had been spinning in circles, making herself dizzy, when she fell on the tines of a garden rake. Her leg was bleeding badly from a large gash. No one was home and Marn did not know where the hospital was. In the ensuing hysteria, Marn sent Linda to get the Welcome Wagon lady — who had taken a shine to the family when she first met them — to drive them to the hospital, with Linda and Susan in the rumble seat and Polly wailing in Marn's lap, her leg bandaged with a Kotex, all Marn could find that was large enough to stop the bleeding. (For the record, Polly had 36 stitches.) So it was lucky that Marnie had such an outgoing way about her, and the special magic of her family got her through.

Polly

So in her short life, Marn had gone from the comfortable home of her birth to the wildly dysfunctional one of Aunt Mary and Aunt Rose, then into a promising marriage and out the other side, at the age of 29, to single motherhood with three little children. She had almost no prospects, and despite promises to the contrary, Ted was sparing and inconsistent with his financial support. It was 1940 and there were not a lot of options for a woman in her position. She often found herself forced to rely on others, which is something she hated with a vengeance. For the most part, her pluck and ingenuity were all she had. That and her three daughters. You will soon see that this was all she needed, but at the time, she had no idea how they would manage. And so she continued to press on, looking for a way to provide them all with a life.

PART TWO

Eventually, Marn was somehow able to finagle them all a house, on Plain Road in Wayland, moving them in late winter of 1943. It was very old and drafty, with a wood-burning stove in the kitchen. Which would have been fun except that there was no one to chop, stack or haul any wood. The bit of firewood they had got them through the first couple of months, but they had run out by mid-March, and after that they were cold quite a lot. When Linda and Susan got home from school, the girls would turn on the radio and listen to Captain Midnight or whatever was on, all of them huddled under the covers in Marn's bed for warmth until it was dinnertime, when they would dash to the kitchen, often sitting in front of the open oven door.

Midge and her girls.

Midge had found work as a telephone operator. These were the days when one needed an operator in order to make a call, and there were but a handful of women in all working the switchboard, taking both day and night shifts, connecting calls in the town. It was a good job for a woman without secretarial or teaching skills, but it meant longs hours. And it was impossible to get time off for any but the weightiest of reasons. The other operators would have been happy to cover for her occasionally, as she would have for them, but the supervisors could be a little hard-boiled, at least at first. So the three Robinson girls ended up being on their own sometimes, with 8-year-old Linda in charge. At first Marn only worked night shifts, so the girls washed the dinner dishes and put themselves to bed while she worked. It is said that Linda was unusually responsible at a very young age, but this can't have sat well with Marn.

Still she was so elated, not just to have a place of their own, but also to get out from under her older, judgmental sister. Nana, for all her charming ways, could be biting when plastered, and took occasional drunken chances to remind Midge of her charity in taking them all in. And Dick was becoming more loathsome and vulgar around the girls, so Marnie felt she better get them out of there.

But her haste to cut her dependence on one sister ended up getting her in hot water with the other one, as Marn borrowed some of the money to make the deposit on the place from Sissy. This was the first of several bad calls where Sissy was concerned, as she and her husband Bill could be judgmental when it came to his sister-in-law Midge. Bill Bartel didn't see why he should have to contribute to the care of Ted's kids. And Sissy was just kind of mean. But Marn did what she could, and the house on Plain Road, tumbledown though it was, was a tremendous turning point for Marn and her young family.

She became friendly with a few of the people who lived nearby. Down the road was an older couple who sat on their front porch a lot. The Donovans were every bit as Irish as Marn, and Frank Donovan would sing a cheery good morning to her in his brogue, while Frank's wife Mim waved a lacy little hankie, every time she passed their small house. Between work and chores and child rearing, there was not a lot of spare time, so she never got to know them very well, but Midge Robinson just couldn't help making friends. And I'm sure it was good to know that there were folks nearby who might help if Polly were to chop off her leg or something.

The house on Plain Road was so ramshackle, Marnie must have made some sort of deal with whoever owned it, because it was probably not up to standards for inhabitability, and they did not stay there very long. For the girls though, it is remembered as having been a great adventure. It was sort of like camping for them, and they were too young to know that they were poor or in any way disadvantaged. For Marn it represented a stepping-stone on the way to making a suitable life for her daughters.

Since she knew they were not going to stay there for long, she did not furnish it except for the bare minimum, adding to the camping adventure feel of the place for the children. She cleaned it to within an inch of its life, however, and she did hang little gingham curtains made from dishtowels in the sparkling kitchen windows. It was a small gesture, a way to make her mark on the big old barn. One has to imagine that every little thing she could do to make life seem normal was comforting for her, even hanging kitchen curtains to make a shack feel like a proper home for three little girls.

Most of the girls' growing up years were spent in a little house on Millbrook Road in Wayland, a sweet clapboard cottage with a screened porch and two bedrooms. They had yards on either side of the house, with iris and day lilies in the spring and purple phlox in the summer. Marn even bought some second-hand furniture, including a bright yellow sofa that turned out to be too big to fit through the door from the back hall into the living room. The deliveryman brought it as far as the side door, leaving it to the family to do the rest. They all huffed and puffed, pushing it through the back door and down the hall toward the living room, but it wouldn't make the corner. They stood back, looked at each other, and burst into snickers, and the sofa stayed as far into the house as it got, which blocked the bathroom door so that anyone wanting to use the bathroom had to climb over it. Sitting in it put you half in the kitchen though, so it was well used and stayed like that for all the years they lived there – everyone would forget about the strangeness of it until a new person came to call, and then they would all have another good laugh over it.

In a lot of ways, this house represented another real step in the right direction for the family, but it was in one way a huge added burden for Marn; it was very far from town. She wanted so badly to get a decent house for them, but couldn't afford the rents in town. So, where she had been less than a mile from work when they lived on Plain Road, now she was a good two miles from the telephone company, a distance she had to cover on foot, both ways, day and night and in every kind of weather. I can hardly imagine — knowing Marn in later life as I did as a lady who lived in the center of town and drove a brand-new yellow station wagon with air conditioning and wood paneling on the side — that she could ever have had to walk two miles to and from work. But back then she was doing what she had to do for her children, with very few resources beyond her own wits.

This is not something she ever even talked about with Linda, Susan and Polly. They really had very little awareness that she was enduring this hardship, or that it was a hardship at all, until they were adults looking back. They remember her leaving the house as though she were off to go sledding. She sometimes skipped for a while as they watched her go. The fact that she was able to give so enthusiastically to them in the evenings – when all she wanted to do was put her feet up, I'm sure – is at the heart of what made her unique. It also bolsters her claims about being a basketball star in high school – the girl had stamina.

This house was almost as drafty as the last one, with an ancient coal furnace in the cellar that did not seem to work – not that they could afford the coal. There was a fireplace too, but firewood was not much cheaper than coal. They might have suffered through another freezing winter, but a most unlikely hero rescued them from that particular fate. An elderly man named Mr. Walker came by the house one day shortly after they moved in. He was stooped and gaunt but gentlemanly, and offered to deliver wood to them for burning in their fireplace for a very low price. After he left, the four of them all giggled over how ancient he seemed to be – how could he ever heft wood around? They giggled even more when he returned the next day in an equally ancient truck and began bringing the firewood into the screened porch… one log at a time. It took hours upon hours for him to finish the job, but finish it he did, and they used the fireplace almost every night in the winter months.

Marn slept in the smaller bedroom downstairs, and the girls slept upstairs in what was really a sort of modified attic – one big room with stairs at one end. There wasn't much furniture in the room; just some shelves and a chifforobe and three beds set up so the children could see one another. In cold weather, the warmth from the fireplace went up the staircase like a chimney, so the room was always cozy and warm at bedtime. At night, the three girls would get into their beds, singing in harmony and playing little games of their own invention – that seem to defy description – until Marn yelled up to them to knock it off. By morning, there was sometimes frost on the windows but Marn would have been up before them getting the fire stoked up so it was a good idea to get up and dressed and downstairs quickly. I don't think I can say that Marnie invented this technique by which she got the girls to bed at night and up in the morning – and it would only work in cold weather, which it wasn't always – but one imagines that it did the trick.

31

The house was situated close enough to the elementary school that the girls could walk to and from school each day, and they entered the first, second and third grades that fall. With the occasional exception of Polly, they were well-behaved in school, which was a good thing because Marn could never get time off to visit with teachers, or even go to the pageants or other school programs. This tore at her, and she would always ask a million questions at dinner the next night. Sometimes they would have a re-creation of the event, featuring whichever daughter had been in the program, with her sisters filling in the parts played by others. Marn would clap her hands to her mouth in an exaggerated state of rapture – brows arching up and a look of pure enjoyment across her face.

One of the few times she insisted on being excused from a shift was when Susan had a solo in the fifth-grade pageant. The girls came flying home that day, all of them a-twitter over Susan's accomplishment. They were so excited to tell their mother – it was as though they had all three gotten the solo. And when they told Marnie, she too became a part of it. They were a package deal.

Susan

Susan was singing "Nearer my God to Thee." She wore a white dress, her big sister's white gloves from Aunt Rose days, and brand new little white socks, and Marn would not have missed that day for anything, as I'm sure her supervisor recognized. She arrived that rainy day in her coat and purse and clear plastic rain bonnet that folded up into a tiny thing, and sort of slipped along the walls of the school's front hallway, trying to be unobtrusive. But Linda's friend Susan Colliton saw her and ran over, making a stir. The school's principal came up then and introduced himself, taking the opportunity to tell her how lovely her daughters were. Unprepared for speaking to anyone, and as excited as she was, she babbled something that she could not even remember later, and is said to have sat in the back of the auditorium and cried through the whole performance.

Each daughter's experience in school was unique, owing to their different personalities. Linda was polite and serious, rather like a little grown-up, always helping the teacher hand things out. Polly was just the opposite, getting into fights in the schoolyard – she wore a brace and funny shoes to correct her clubfoot, for which she often got taunted. Being as scrappy as she was, she did not take much of this, and her big sisters often had to rescue her from dust-ups at recess.

Susan's experience was classically Susan. Early on in that second-grade year, she raised her hand to ask the teacher whether, since the soil on Earth was called earth, the soil on Mars was called mars. The teacher laughed at her, telling her it was a silly question. Susan was dumbfounded! She thought (all her life, I might add) that it was a pretty damn smart question, but the experience kept her from asking as many questions as she might have otherwise, in school at least.

They were a pack, Marnie and her daughters. They were as close as any family ever was. I have no doubt that Marn actively fostered the bond among her three daughters, as they had to rely on one another when she was at work. And although I was not there, I have heard enough of the stories, all my life, to know that there was something very special about this family, growing up. There was an aura about their home that made all the girls' friends want to come home with them after school, even though the house was plain to the point of shabbiness, with a big sofa stuck in the back hallway that blocked the bathroom. Clearly, it wasn't the house or their possessions; it was Marn!

The love that poured out of her – that aura – came to land on anyone who came near. And it was the fun. Let me tell you, as poor as they were, they had fun. To hear the stories, it is easy to forget that life was a struggle at all, so much fun was had. Their brand of fun did not consist of dinners out or vacations or the circus, but rather just getting a kick out of everyday life. They sang together constantly, in three-part harmony, which they always said made washing dishes go by much faster. They regaled each other at the dinner table with funny stories of their days. Simple fun. One time, they painted the back door on a whim. They had all set to cleaning out a little shed at the back of the house. Most of the contents had been there when they moved in, including three small cans of paint and three paintbrushes. Marn gave them each a brush and a can, and they went wild on the back door, the results of which had to be hidden from the landlord. He lived right across the street, but thankfully he always came to the front door.

Fun just hid around every corner; on any given day, Marn might, for instance, enter the living room full of school chums by flinging herself over the couch in a modified handspring, and land sitting down as though nothing strange had occurred. If anyone was to make a comment, she would say, "I'm sure I have no idea what you are talking about, my dear," which just made the gaggle of girls giggle even more. Public displays like this sometimes mortified her daughters, but all their friends just ate it up.

She always took an interest in the other children that came to call. She would ask one child where her freckles came from, or whether the teacher knew how much another child giggled. "Isn't that marvelous!" was her response to the girl whose father was a mortician. Naturally, the other children loved the attention, but they also loved the closeness of the family.

Often they were envious of this little gang, poor and fatherless though they were.

By virtue of her job at the telephone company, Marn became a conduit of information and a confidante (she was very good at keeping secrets), as people in town came to know her. They would leave messages with her for others, and she always had a word of greeting. Once in a while she even stood in as a baby sitter, when a mother would call to say she was leaving the phone off the hook while she ran next door, and would Midge listen for the baby.

By virtue of her personality, she garnered many friends and admirers – people were just drawn to her easy, funny style. She was even invited to parties at the homes of the telephone company managers, which I'm sure she loved, being as social as she was. She would sometimes borrow a dress from one of the other operators, as she only owned one or two dressy numbers, and they were mostly for church. The girls would watch in fascination as their mother went from a workaday mom to a cocktail party lady, complete with makeup – which she wore very sparingly in those days owing to the expense – and jewelry. She had some of her mother's jewelry, and some that Ted had given her. She would even wear fancy hose, which she put on carefully and then took off the minute she got home so as to make them last to the next invitation. She would come home at the ends of these evenings singing and laughing, always in fine spirits – probably owing to the fine spirits that were served at the parties – and the girls would try to wait up for her so they could hear all the delicious details of the houses, the guests and especially the food.

These were the days, however, when a woman did not get divorced, much less work nights as a telephone operator. And after a while, Marn began to sense that the wives of those telephone company managers were threatened by her presence, a divorcee – and especially such a lively one, who drank freely and spoke her mind – in the midst of their cocktail parties (and their husbands). She didn't want to create problems or cause tongues to wag, but she had so few opportunities to socialize. The parties had been a great respite from her life of work and children and poverty. Although it must have nearly killed her to do so, she stopped accepting the invitations, making up excuses until they finally stopped coming.

When old Mr. Walker died, her source for firewood dried up, and she had to find a new way to heat their home. She asked around, but everyone else's prices were much higher, even the husband of one of the other operators, who told her he'd give her a break. She got a little flustered when he quoted such a prohibitively high price, and was momentarily unable to think of what to say (she'd say she "got the apple"), but then blurted something out to try and get out of having to say she couldn't afford it.

"Well, that is very kind of you, Andy," she smiled, "but what I really want to do is get the coal furnace going. It's so much more convenient."

The girls were standing nearby, and exchanged looks of utter surprise. What was she talking about?? She always said they could not afford to fix the furnace, and that's why they used firewood.

Midge finished up her conversation with Andy and spun around to leave, spinning them all around too, but not before they each got a chance to glare at her. As they walked home, Susan started to ask about the conversation about the furnace.

Before she got more than three words out, Marn turned abruptly and said, "I will not have my children questioning me! None of that now! Run on ahead, and get started on your homework."

That evening, a car pulled in the driveway. It was Andy Thompson's son Jeff who, it turns out, was just getting started as an apprentice fixing furnaces. She welcomed him in and showed him the door to the cellar. He smiled and waved at the girls, who stood as a block, saying nothing.

Jeff got the furnace going for a very nominal fee, and filled the coal bin to brimming for free. The girls were so happy to have heat coming out of the registers, they did not think much more about how she had made it happen, at least not right away. At some point, they all wondered. Had she lied? Had she used her feminine wiles on Andy Thompson? The girls never asked, partly out of respect for her, but also I think they didn't want to know. And they didn't want to force Marn's hand by making her own up to a misdeed.

Marnie was a fighter – a tough lady – and she would be damned if she could not provide her girls with whatever was in her power. Beyond a roof and heat, this did not amount to much in those years, and over the years the three girls shared school clothes and prom dresses and sometimes, much less enthusiastically, the infrequent Sunday roast, when someone would come to call and be invited to join the family for dinner. And since our Midge was so popular and sought after, people often came to call. But the Sunday afternoon callers were the worst, as this meant that the meal the girls had smelled cooking all day, their mouths watering as the afternoon wore on, would have to be stretched to accommodate the extra mouth.

The lesson learned was not so much about sharing as it was about manners – if someone arrives at your house as dinner is being served, it is only polite to ask them to dinner. "Oh, Mr. O'Rourke, it's you! Well, don't just stand there looking like a fool, come on in with you!" The only consolation was that the dinner would be enhanced by the addition of someone fun, or if he or she was dreadful, dinner the next night would be spent giggling about how they had gotten through dinner the night before.

Midge Robinson had definite ideas on how to raise her girls. She never seemed to waver or lose her focus. It was like she was working from a handbook. She employed a firm but fair hand and taught them by example (with the very rare and untalked-about exception) how to get the most out of life. There were many important lessons to be learned, mostly in the form of wisdom to be passed on. Her daughters knew just how she felt on most subjects pertaining to them, and woe betide the child who transgressed.

Manners were important. The girls were expected to be ladies at all times. Little Miss Polly was the toughest to keep in line, but a lot was expected of them all. They were to stand when an elder entered the room, and always look people in the eye. They wore dresses to school every day, and Marn braided each girl's hair before school. To see the girls in their classrooms, one would never know how their mother struggled to put food on the table and clothes on their backs. It's not so much that appearances mattered to Marn, but she felt so strongly about giving her daughters the best possible chance in life. There was an expectation about how a child ought to be dressed for school and she felt that deviating from it might take away from their chances to be taken seriously or encouraged.

There were chores to be done when Linda, Susan and Polly got home, and as you know, they often had to fend for themselves when their mother was working. But much of the time the chores coincided with family time, so it might include singing or talking about things, making the work almost seem like fun.

One of their responsibilities, on the days when Marn worked the evening shift, was to keep that temperamental coal-burning furnace going in the cellar, but one night the girls accidentally let the pilot light go out. This was a very serious transgression, as it meant Marn would have to stay up late to re-light it and wait for the fire to get established when she got home from work.

Before they went to bed, the girls cleaned out the ashes, laid a new fire of newspapers and wood, filled the coal bucket and set Marn's sherry bottle and glass at the top of the cellar stairs, along with a little note, explaining what had happened. One can only imagine Marnie's reaction to that small still life upon arriving home.

It was difficult for the girls, with no car and a mother that worked, getting to visit friends. Fortunately for Linda, she had one very good friend, Susan Colliton, living just a few houses down, so she had someone to play with after school. It was hardest for Sue, none of whose school friends lived nearly. And there was not much Marn could do about it. But they all had each other – they were kind of stuck with each other. And, as much as Susan might have liked to have her own friend in the neighborhood, she was something of a loner anyway, often content to sit in the top of a pine tree watching the clouds, or reading on the sofa.

Linda was the serious one, everyone says, and being the oldest, she took on the role of enforcer of the rules as her mother had laid them down. In addition, Linnie devised some rules of her own. For example, they were not to bring up bad news when Marnie came home from work – Linda seems to have had some inkling of what it was like for her mother, and endeavored to make life easier in any way she could.

It was, not surprisingly, Polly who most often violated this rule. She would solemnly promise all afternoon to keep mum on something or other, and then blurt it out the minute Marnie walked through the door. Or she would take it upon herself to "help," by doing something like lighting the gas hot water heater so she could have a bath. This she attempted one day, leaving the gas on while she went off in search of a match. When she returned and struck the match, a thunderous cloud of gas lit up the cellar, singeing Polly's eyebrows off. Not something you can easily hide when Mother returns home, even if you were inclined to lie, which Linda most definitely was not.

Susan, the middle child, was the pretty one, Marnie's designation. (Linda was the smart one; Polly the funny one.) And Susan was certainly adorable, with blond curls and the most angelic face – she was downright cherubic. She was so beautiful as a child that, when she was hospitalized at about age 3 for colitis – and almost died – the hospital took photos of her being tended to by a doctor and nurse and used them in a magazine about the hospital.

Sue was rarely in trouble, if you don't count the time she got her arm caught in the washing machine wringer. All by herself in the cellar, trying to be helpful, she got herself so that she could not free her sleeve and her arm was stuck. Sure that it was going to chop her arm clean off, and unaccustomed to danger as she was, it was a harrowing experience for her, so it was to her credit that she continued to help with the laundry after that.

Marn was hard on Susan, more so than the other two. If you ask me, being labeled "the pretty one" was a strike against her from the start. Marn cautioned her as a child against becoming conceited, which I think dove straight to her soul from that moment on and stayed with her throughout her life. It's just like the remark from her second grade teacher about her question being stupid; when you told Susan something about herself, she took it straight to the bank, living the rest of her life based on what may well have been an off-handed comment.

One wonders what Susan could have become if she were not treated as third best. Not that she wasn't wonderful just as she was, but you wish (and I think she did too) that she could have had a little more encouragement from old Marn.

And Polly, as I've said, was the funny one. The baby of the family, she was forever misbehaving, clowning around boisterously and generally looking for fun – which often meant trouble – any way she could find it. As a toddler, she was supposed to be having a nap one day, and when Marn went in to get her up, she had covered her face with diaper rash ointment, and then gotten into the baby powder. Marn loved to recount how she opened the door to find Polly sitting on the floor with a white clown-face, powder in her hair and all over her clothes, and a look of pure angelic innocence on her face. She was a problem child, right from the start.

They all occasionally got in trouble with the landlord, who unfortunately lived right across the street. He missed most of their antics, but occasionally they did something right under his nose, like climbing out of their bedroom window at night onto the little roof created by the bay window in the living room. They thought they were so sneaky, hiding from Marn up there, and would have a gay old time chatting and singing in the twilight and tearing off little bits of the roofing shingles, tossing them out into the gathering dark as Marn sat downstairs, reading the newspaper and listening to the radio. But the landlord had only to look out his front window to see them, crammed onto this small roof in their nightgowns, giggling and hooting like a trio of sweet little ghosties. As always, the worst part of getting caught was facing

Marnie with the knowledge that they had disappointed her. She did not have many rules, but staying out of trouble was one of them.

Eating together was important too. When she worked nights, they often sat down to dinner at 3:30 in the afternoon so that Marn could make the walk to work for 6:00. Then after dinner, they would busy themselves with clean-up, homework and early to bed, where they would continue to talk and sing together in the little bunkroom they all shared. When she worked the day shift, it was their job to have dinner, if not on the table, then at least well on its way, by the time their mother got home. So all the girls learned to be good cooks – Marnie's wonderful recipes went from Linda to Susan, and on down the line to Polly – they really never saw meal preparation as a chore in those days, but more as something fun to do together. That is pure Marnie.

The children got along very well, considering they were all girls and very close in age. And, as serious and mature as she was, Linnie could often be found playing with Polly. The two would pretend that they were on a ship, or at school or at work in an office. They would build forts in the living room out of pillows and blankets, all while Susan lay on the sofa, her usual spot. Susan was decidedly low-energy, and so her role in the made-up games was almost always the part of "Sick Sister Theresa on the Couch." So when Polly and Linda were busy being pirates, spies or cowboys, there was always a part for Sue too.

They were also all enrolled in Sunday school, each girl attending right through confirmation. The teachings there fell on completely deaf ears when it came to Polly and Linda, but Susan took to it enthusiastically. She became so fervent on the topic that she began to talk of becoming a nun. Which is very funny when you think of Sue in later years, smoking and drinking and swearing. She even told some of us, in a case of way too much information, how much she enjoyed sex, and that her husband had built their bed to a particular height for the purpose of their lovemaking. Methinks she would have made a very unusual nun.

It should be said that there was teasing and sibling squabbles from time to time. Even Linda – the responsible, serious one – scared Polly out of her wits one night by hiding outside the bedroom window with Susan Colliton. They disguised their voices to sound like men and held a mock discussion about whether or not to "murder the little one tonight." I'm glad to know that my mother wasn't always playing the role of mature mother figure, but was able to find a way to act like a typical kid from time to time.

One day when the girls were around 7, 9 and 11, they had finished their homework and put on their coats to spend the last few hours of daylight in the yard. One by one, they kissed Marn and headed out into the windy afternoon. Susan, who would have preferred to stay indoors, began quietly searching the ground for pebbles and colored glass to add to a small, non-descript collection she was compiling on the brick wall at the edge of the driveway. Studiously, she frowned at the ground, bending to pick up a tiny stone, barely bigger than a fingernail, and turned it over in her hand. If she felt the stone had some merit – an interesting shape, perhaps, or a pretty color – she'd place it alongside the others. Her favorite find was a larger piece that she swore was in the perfect shape of a dog. She often just sat, admiring her collection, occasionally picking up one piece or another to hold up to the light or rub on a sleeve.

Polly and Linda were earnestly trying to build a fort in the corner of the side yard by the chimney. They had found some boards under the porch, and were using these in an industrious, if futile, attempt to create a frame by balancing them against one another and the chimney bricks. They would get the whole thing to balance, and then shore the lumber up with sticks jammed into the lawn.

"Oh, Linnie! Linnie! Polly!" The call came from Susan at the front of the house, with an excited urgency the other two rarely heard coming from their sister. They turned, not caring that their fort sagged slowly to the ground as soon as they let go of its posts, and hurried through the fallen leaves around the side of the house. There, standing very close to Susan was a large-ish black dog.

"Where did he come from?" asked Linda, as Polly raced past.

"I don't know, I just looked up and he was there."

"He doesn't look like he belongs to anyone," said Polly, trying to sound knowledgeable and grown up, when really she was overcome with delight at finding the tufted mutt in their very own yard. She pushed her hair, and the few leaves tangled in it out of her eyes in the breeze and got down on her knees in the grass.

"Let's call him Fluffy," said Susan, who would rather have found a kitten.

"Actually, I think he's a she," said Linda. Susan allowed as how the name really worked either way.

"Let's see if she knows anything," said Polly, "Come on, girl, come." The dog obligingly ambled over to Polly, who patted the top of its head with a mittened hand. Fluffy wagged her tail like a flag and licked Polly's nose.

"Girls!" Marnie called out, cranking open the kitchen window, "Be careful! You don't know if he's friendly!"

"It's a girl and we named her Fluffy," called Susan in response.

"No we didn't, Sue," said Linda, "we haven't decided." And then to her mother, she said, "She seems pretty nice, Mom, she really does."

"Well, just be careful," said Marn as she began to crank the window closed again, "I don't need any daughters with missing arms or legs." Before the window shut completely, she called out again, giving them ten more minutes before it was time to come in for supper.

The three of them spent those last minutes of outside time happily playing with their new friend, putting a string around her uncollared neck and leading her around like a pony.

When at last it was time to go inside, they said their goodbyes to the young dog, hating to leave those big friendly eyes and slowly wagging tail. As soon as they were inside, all three ran to the window to see if she was still there – which she was – and the dinner table conversation that night was of nothing but the dog.

"Do you think we could keep her?" asked Linda

"I think she's got a little wolf in her," gushed Polly, "but not in a scary way. It just makes her very brave." Marn did her best to quash their enthusiasm, pointing out that she probably belonged to someone. "But who, Mom? We know everyone for miles around," they all said, stumbling over each other, "The Bennetts have Amos and Luther, and the Hutchinsons have Ribsy, and I don't think the Sawyers have a dog at all! Oh, please, Mom? Oh, Puulleease?"

"I, for one, do not care for begging," said Marn, indicating that was all she'd say on the subject, which was enough to get all three to clamp their mouths shut.

Later that evening, after the children had been put to bed, Marn sat down to read the newspaper, but not before looking out the front window to see if the dog was still there. She was. In truth, Marn would have liked nothing more than to keep the dog. It was quite a beauty – a Belgian Shepherd mix, it has since been decided – and it would be a comfort to have a dog around the house when she was out at work. Still, she did not need another mouth to feed, and the landlord – who, you will remember, lived right across the street – was firm in his rules, and no dogs was one of them.

The next day was Saturday, and the girls were up at the crack of dawn, running to the windows to look for their new friend. There she was, lying in the grass by the side of the driveway, her nose resting on her front paws. You never saw those girls get dressed so fast – faster than you could say Jack Robinson, as Marn would say – and like three little flashes, they were out the door to shower the pup with affection. When Marn called them in for breakfast, she marveled at their rosy cheeks and buoyant spirits.

She had made her decision already, as she had lain in bed the night before – there was not much she could give the girls by way of special toys and such, but here was an opportunity to make them very happy. Still, she spent breakfast trying to talk them out of it, with admonishments about the many chores that would be added to their already-long lists, but it was clear, not surprisingly, that nothing would deter her daughters in their enthusiasm. When at last she gave them the good news, the first thing out of Linda's mouth was a definitive statement about the dog's name. "We can't call her Fluffy," she declared, "That's a cat's name, and besides, she's really not fluffy. More like silky."

"And black," added Polly.

And so it was that Blackie came to live with the family. She was a wonderful addition, dearly loved, and she sweetly endured dress-up afternoons and hiding upstairs with the girls whenever the landlord (and once, even the dogcatcher) came by.

Shortly after her arrival, Blackie took to waiting at the corner for her three mistresses to get out of school every day, walking them proudly home. She did the same thing for Marnie when she worked nights. Marn would come out of the phone company building, and there would be Blackie to walk with her to the small unassuming house they all called home.

There was much consternation in the household when Blackie vanished for several days once. The girls were frantic; even Marn went out looking for her. When Blackie finally came home, she was in a state of agitation, and somehow convinced her entire family to follow her to a cave in the woods way behind the house, where she had a litter of pups. Linda ran back to the house and found a cardboard box, and the litter was transported home, where the girls marveled to watch the mother dog care for her young. The

Blackie and the Robinson girls.

jovial young milkman took an interest in adopting one of them, and the girls told him he could have one of the puppies for free if he would marry their mother. He reported this deal to Marn, who found it very funny, but suggested to them in a little chat that evening that it was not necessary for them to find her a husband. She had no time for one anyway, she said.

There was at least one neighbor who had eyes for our hero Midge; a formal, dapper gentleman by the name of Mr. Clemons. In his hat and gloves, he would walk by frequently on his way to town, always stopping to say hello. One day, Marn was washing the windows, sitting on the sill as she reached out to clean the outside glass, while the girls busied themselves with the inside. Along came Mr. Clemons, strolling into the yard in his finery. Formality required a handshake and, seemingly unaware of the precariousness of her perch, he extended his gloved hand to her. She switched the vinegar bottle to the other hand – the one holding the window — and extended her hand to him. Inside, the girls watched first in horror, then fascination, as her legs rose up into the air, and she balanced as if my magic, shaking his hand and making pleasantries even as she was nearly falling out of the window. As he strode away, Marnie righted herself, leaned in the window for a moment, and said, "I think, sometimes, that our Mr. Clemens is a bit in the ether." She winked at them, ducked her head, and went back to being just a pair of legs hanging down through the front bay window.

While nothing ever happened between Marn and Mr. Clemens, Bill Edwards was another story entirely. He was a businessman, happily married, who traveled a lot, and managed over the course of many years to arrange his itinerary so that he could stop every so often and pay a visit to the house where Midge lived. He was by all accounts a wonderful man, and the girls loved his visits. They'd all laugh and have fun, eat supper and play games together until it was time for the children to go to bed. It was such fun to have someone else in the little house, and to see Marn so animated. The next morning, he'd still be there, having coffee in the kitchen when the girls came down the stairs. Their youth prevented any of them from wondering what had gone on after they'd gone to bed, but they have pieced it together in later years, adding it to the crazy quilt of their mother's life. Although I'm sure we don't know of all the lovers she had, we are aware of some pretty interesting stories. Marnie seems to have lived much of her life outside convention in this area, as she did in so many others. This is what I meant by her not caring so much about social mores – the formalities of relationships – caring more about, well, caring. And fun. And love.

Although she stayed mum on the subject of the men in her life, Marn was very open with her daughters in almost every other arena. She saw little reason to shield her children from life or lie to them. I'm sure the circumstances of her own life played a part in this.

When the girls were in their early teen years, Marn sat them down on a Saturday morning.

"I think you girls are old enough now for this," she told them, "You know we're having trouble making ends meet." The girls all nodded solemnly. They knew Marn was barely getting by, although it sometimes seemed unfair that they couldn't have the things their classmates had. Even back then, kids could be ruthless in their teasing, and all three girls had felt at one time or another the sting of a schoolyard joke.

"I think it's time you had a real understanding of how this all works," she went on, "Starting today, I'm putting you three in charge of paying the bills."

The girls looked at each other in amazement, and then at Marn, not believing what she had said.

"You will take turns, each month. Linnie, we'll start with you."

Not surprisingly, small sighs of relief could be heard coming from the other two, and they pulled their chairs up to the little kitchen table to watch their older sister be indoctrinated into the world of the family finances. Marn brought a pile of envelopes to the table, and spread the bills in front of Linda. She then gave Linda a number representing the sorry amount of money there was that month, after buying food, to pay said bills. A quick, rough computation in her head told Linda that there was not enough to pay all of them. Just the rent alone would take up almost all of it, and then there was the telephone, and the electric bill, and the gas bill – feeling a little frantic, she looked up at Marn.

"Mom, there's not enough. How can we pay the bills?" Marn smiled a sad smile; as much as she felt that her daughters needed to know this, she felt also a twinge of pain at Linda's realization.

"Well, now, it's important to pay the rent," she explained gently, "and all these others have to get something too. Now, you must figure out how much each one gets."

Linda sat with those bills for a long time before she returned them, red-faced, to Marnie. Marn stroked her hair, saying crisply, "Thank you, sweetie! That's a big help."

"But how will we get by?" Linda whispered, "I'm scared."

"Oh, lovey, don't be frightened," Marn cooed, her voice a mix of soothing and frankness, "We've got each other, and we've got a lot of love. We may not have a lot of money, but we've got a lot, haven't we?" Linda nodded.

"Things will get better, sweetie. They will. You'll see." She kissed Linda on her cheek and took the bills into the other room.

And that's the way it went. Polly was still a little too young to fully grasp the task, so Linda helped her when it was her turn, but gradually the girls became comfortable with their bill-paying system. They quickly learned which bills could be put off – they never even thought of paying a bill in full — and they were twice as appreciative of all expenditures on themselves, especially the money that was set aside so that they could ride their bikes to Higgins's Dairy Barn once a month for ice cream sundaes. In fact, the ritual of bill paying became to take on a festive tone, the girls taking pleasure in managing the bills down to the penny. They began to take their ride to Higgins's as soon as the bills were paid, calling the outing "money-done sundaes." It is a wonder, looking back, that Marn made it through those years without going to jail.

Around this time, the long-lost Ted Robinson showed up one day. He was single again. (Some say he figured out that the baby wasn't his, and never married the other woman at all.) The girls were astounded to see him, as was their mother. He had been almost completely missing, save a few cards that occasionally contained a small amount of money, for the better part of ten years. Midge was even more astonished when he told her he had made a big mistake and that he still loved her and would like to make it up to her, move back in and marry her again. How she must have struggled in her heart and mind! On the one hand, he had some nerve to come around after the lurch he'd left her in. But at the same time, his proposal represented a better, or at least more comfortable life for them all.

When he left that day, Marn called a family meeting and laid her cards on the table. Their father had asked to come and live with them. They would no longer be poor, she told them; everything would be paid for. Since the girls

51

had been doing the bills at this point, they knew the realities of their financial situation. They chatted about it for a while, but still two of the three said no. They knew that, as much as she had loved him once upon a time, Marnie didn't want him back. He had broken her heart and left her to fend for herself, and while the children did not know all the details, they had an inkling that he had done something bad. Polly (did you guess?) was the holdout. Of the four women living in that house, there was but one who held a sweet spot in her heart for Ted, and that was Polly. Having been too little to remember the pain the family had gone through, she still saw him as her big strong handsome father, and secretly (or not-so-secretly) had a little worship thing going on with him. One would have to assume that Ted was cognizant of this, and so he continued to write to her, even though she did acquiesce on the subject of his moving back in, and his proposal was turned down.

Ironically, it was that Christmas that Marn asked Sissy and her husband for some special, and rather expensive corrective shoes for Polly. This was misstep number two: Bill Bartel turned her down, saying it was the responsibility of the girl's father to buy these things for her. It was a nasty exchange, leaving Marn feeling left out in the cold. Plus, she could not afford to buy the shoes, so Polly went without.

The clubfoot could not be ignored however, so when Polly was 13, she was sent to Murphy Army Hospital for another surgery. Marn had researched surgeons, asking around of friends and associates, and settled on a doctor located at this particular Waltham, Mass facility. As they still did not have a car, Sissy drove Polly to the hospital — Marnie couldn't even get the time off from work to go along. She was in a state of pure agony as she watched her sister's car pull away, with Polly's anguished face visible in the window until the car turned the corner. Polly really kind of hated her aunt Sissy, and was frightened to the core at being away from her mother, but there was simply no choice in the matter. Even after her surgery — she had to stay in the hospital for a month — she saw Marn a total of three times, as the only way Marn could get to the hospital was a series of bus rides that basically took all day. This was so very hard on Marnie, and Polly always made it ten times worse by shrieking and banging on her bed as her mother was leaving, yelling, in a wild, clenched-teeth style most unbecoming a young lady, "Don't you leave me! Don't you leave me!" One evening, a nurse stopped her as she was walking out. Marn was dabbing her eyes with a hankie from her raincoat pocket, trying to fight back the tears. The older nurse put her hand on Marnie's arm. "She'll be fine," she said soothingly. "As soon as you're gone, within five minutes, she calms right down."

"I don't know if you are trying to make me feel better," said Marn, "but it's not working!"

The nurse smiled, nodding. "She is a rascal, that one!"

"That's putting it mildly," said Marn. "I think she's got the devil in her!" (When Marn said devil, it came out sounding like "divil," a bit of homage to her Irish roots.) The two of them chuckled as Marn opened the door to the lobby and was gone.

The Murphy Army Hospital, oddly enough, is where Polly learned to smoke. Her room was at the end of a long hall, and it had windows, so this was where the nurses came to take their cigarette breaks – so hard to imagine in today's world! Not only that the nurses smoked in a patient's room, but that they taught a 14-year-old girl to smoke.

When Polly finally came home, her father came to visit again. Sadly, it does seem that Ted wished to play some part in his daughters' lives, a wish made tragic by his own reprehensible actions, from which there would be no recovery. (No Man Walks Out on Marjorie Robinson.) Still he tried to weasel his way in, the visit to the recuperating Polly being another attempt.

She tried disguising her glee at seeing him, but gave it away with her joyful shout, "Daddy!" He strode in, acknowledging the others as politely as he could despite their stony looks. He kissed Polly on the head and inquired as to her pain.

"Oh, it's nothing," she said, scrambling to a sitting position. "Want to see my incision?" Ted reeled back a little, a look of mild disgust coming over his face. "No, thank you very much, I most certainly do not."

Polly was crestfallen.

He tried to cajole her, tickling her and telling her how pretty she was, but he had erred in Polly's view of fatherliness. A father would want to see my incision, she thought. Insignificant though it may seem, it was a turning point for her, and things were never the same between him and Marn's youngest. Perhaps she had just needed for him to do something that affected her before she would join the others in their anti-Ted club.

Having been in the hospital so long, Polly had missed a lot of school, and still had more recovering to do, so Marn hired a tutor. His name was Pete Goodell – "The Unitarian," Marn used to call him. Pete was older than Polly by four years or so, and was an awkward boy who would break out in nervous sweats with regularity. He quickly became enamored of the Robinson girls, and approached them one by one with romantic intent. He would show up with a handful of flowers one day and present it to one of them, or ask another one to take a walk with him, even asking Polly to a dance. They each put him off, Polly pointing out that she was not only 13 years old, but on crutches. Then they'd all giggle over it at dinner, doing imitations of his agonizing discomfort for Marn's enjoyment. Incredibly, she got to experience Pete's moves for herself, when he at last tried his luck at wooing Marn! Shot down by all four of them, the Unitarian served his term as Polly's tutor and went on his way, never to be heard from again.

In her mid-teens, Polly had a great friend named Allan Emory. To this day, she keeps a framed photo of him in her house. Marn took a special liking to Allan too, and became friendly with his parents.

Allan had a horse, and Polly loved horses. She would jump on her bike after school and ride up to Allan's house, where they would ride double on Dasher's broad back, Polly always in front. "Someday," Marn would say in a faint rebuke of Polly, "that poor boy is going to get to see what it is like to ride a horse by himself."

Polly

Allan and Polly had also developed a common interest in smoking, and kept a pack of Pall Malls hidden on a rafter in the loft of the barn. Once far enough from the house, they would climb down from the horse and smoke at the edge of a big field. That is, until the day they set the field on fire. A stray ash caught some of the dry field grass, and the next thing they knew, a blaze had blown up that they could not contain.

"Get on Dasher! Quick," implored Polly, no newcomer to trouble. Allan climbed onto the horse, pulling Polly up in front of him, and they lit out galloping for home, getting Dasher into his stall just as the fire engines roared past. Allan's mother came flying out the back door, wiping her hands on a dishtowel as her eyes followed the path of the truck past her house and toward the field. As she ran back inside to the telephone, the two youngsters ambled out of the barn, feigning surprise at all the commotion. Neighbors came running by, yelling to each other as they headed in the direction the fire trucks had gone. No one gave a thought to Polly and Allan, let alone suspecting them as having had a part in setting the blaze, especially since they seemed to be as surprised as everyone else at the burning field.

When Polly got home that evening, she waltzed in the door easy as you please, as though nothing had happened. She gamely set the table for dinner and helped to cut up potatoes. Just as they were to sit down to their meal, however, there came a knock at the front door. Nothing good ever came from a knock at the front door, but the girls always got excited anyway. They shut Blackie in the back hall (in case it was the landlord) and raced to the door, opening it to find two firemen standing there.

"Evening, folks," they began, taking off their fire hats, "we'll just take a minute of your time. We're asking if anyone knows anything about the fire at the Emory house."

"Oh, my goodness," gasped Marn, "the Emory's house is on fire?" Polly caught herself just in time, realizing it was better to keep a low profile during this investigation.

"No, ma'am," one of the burly men said, "The fire was in the field behind their house."

Marn looked at her three children, each one with wide eyes and innocent expressions.

"Do any of you know anything about this?" she asked. They shook their heads in unison, two of them in actual honesty.

"Polly, honey, weren't you down there today?" Marn singled her out, and so Polly began to tell the story of the fire, complete with the part where the two innocent children are quietly brushing Dasher in the barn when they hear distant sirens. As she continued the story, however, Polly found she could not look her mother in the eye. Her pace slowed from a fever pitch to that of a child who suddenly realizes she should not be telling this story at all, or at least not with such gusto. The fact is she could simply not lie to Marnie. Eventually the story came to a complete stop. "What happened next?" asked Susan, almost breathless with the drama of the story. For a girl who did not seek out adventure, Susan was still very interested in anything resembling scuttlebutt.

"That was it," said Polly, "I came home."

The firemen had a few words with Marn, asking her to let them know if she heard anything and thanking her for her time, and they took their leave.

Marn called Polly over to the table. Polly looked at her hands. She hung her head. The room went silent except for the clock ticking away on the shelf.

"Polly? Do you have something you want to tell us?" This was Marnie, who knew her youngest daughter only too well. Polly's behavior belied classic contrition, and Marn knew she only had to wait a moment…

"We started the fire," whispered Polly, "Allan and me. By accident." She went on to tell all, the smoking and everything. Marn listened earnestly, and somewhere in there, dinner was served and they all sat down to it.

"First of all, it's 'Allan and I,'" she began. "Polly, I am glad you have told the truth. You should have been truthful with the firemen, and I'm a little cross with you for that. But at least you have told me what happened."

Polly silently hoped for a reprieve in honor of her honesty, but it was not to be. She was made to call the Fire Department and tell them the truth, and then was sent to her room, where she listened as a rousing game of Charades went on in the living room. Later, she was given a lecture from her mother, the gist of which was 'Crime Doesn't Pay,' and told in no uncertain terms not to smoke cigarettes. It is not known whether she contacted Mrs. Emory, or whether Allan ever got in trouble.

It was shortly after this that Marn found them a place they could afford right in the center of town. One side of a little two-family house, the location was great and it was cheap, but a little tight – especially after they tried to move that same big yellow couch into the house. They had a little help this time, from Andy Thompson and his son Jeff of the fixing-of-the-coal-furnace, but even the two of them were

Polly, Linda in background

stumped by that sofa. Attempting to round the corner in the hallway between the two apartments, it seemed that, if they just opened the neighbor's door across the way, they could swing it around by backing it in there a bit. But it was not to be, and the couch got stuck in both doors, between the two apartments, where it stayed for the rest of the week until Andy could recruit another fellow to assist. The family that lived on the other side of the house – the Bandolins – did not mind this, accepting it as funny.

This was a good sign.

Even when the couch was finally moved, both doors were still likely to be left open. The Bandolins were a lot of fun, and made for a convenient way for Marn to have social interaction. They would have dinner together sometimes or just yell back and forth between the two apartments. Mrs. Bandolin looked to Midge as a role model, and she had the makings of the kind of family matriarch that Marn was.

Living in town was much more convenient for Linnie, Susan and Polly – they could get to the store on foot, and there were other friends who lived nearby – and especially for Marn, who had a considerable shorter commute to work now. Marn's house was still the go-to place after school, but the girls also began to join clubs and cliques, moving out into the world in a way they could not when they lived way out on Millbrook Road.

The following summer, Linda got her first job, as a mother's helper for a family with three daughters who summered in the mountains of Randolph, New Hampshire. It was the summer between her sophomore and junior years of high school, and she had a wonderful time. It was also Marn's first taste of one of her birds flying from the nest, but she was thrilled that Linda was getting to have this new experience.

It was in Randolph that Linnie met the man she would later marry; my father, Chris Harris. Chris tells the story how, that summer, he and a bunch of friends were trying to get a neighbor's tennis court in shape so they could play on it. After a bit they were invited inside for iced tea. Another family, the Crosses, had just arrived and were greeting everyone, introducing the person they'd brought up with them to look after their daughters for the summer. This person had been carsick on the trip and said little if anything. She looked awful, my father says, and he guessed her to be at least 30 (she was 16). (It was Linda.) He saw little of her that summer — he was working trails for the Randolph Mountain Club and anyway had his eye on another gal by the name of Martha Stevens.

Susan's first summer job was also as a mother's helper, but the children she took care of were her own cousins, two of the four Bartel children. Sissy and Bill had a summer house in Duxbury, Mass., and they offered to give Susan money toward college to come and babysit the younger kids.

Susan

The strike three of missteps with the Bartels came at the end of that summer, when Marn told Susan that she needed the money to pay bills. This seems harsh to me, and I can tell you that Susan never forgot it, but it was a hallmark of the family that they shared everything. That was how things were done in the Robinson household, but Bill Bartel was furious with her for doing so. He had given the money to Susan for her schooling, and Marn had no right to take it. He put his foot down and forbade his family from having any contact with Midge or her three daughters. (In a defiant move, Sissy and Bill's oldest daughter Julie often snuck over in the family car, stealing visits with them. Marn was to her a rock, someone she could talk to. I think Julie (and all her siblings) secretly wished Marn was their mother, instead of the stern, unforgiving Sissy.)

Meanwhile, Chris Harris started college at Yale that fall. During Christmas vacation at home, he was dispatched to Concord one snowy night to fetch his sister Edie home from a dance. When he met up with her inside the dance hall, as he tells it, she was accompanied by another very attractive girl. "Chris, you remember Linda Robinson from last summer," she said. (Chance meeting number 2.) He said hello, and brought Edie home. The next summer, back in Randolph, a cousin of his organized a dinner dance one night, inviting Linda, who was again employed by the Crosses. (In Randolph, Linda was known as "Robbie," a shortening of her last name, to differentiate her from Linda Cross, one of the children in her care), Chris drove Linda to the Waumbec House — a quiet, homey little establishment in Jefferson named for an old Indian — for the dance. She was supposed to be his date, and he reports having had a fine time. Robbie, he says, was a wonderful dance partner and they seemed to have a lot to talk about. He drove her home to the Cross house, and they spontaneously kissed. Despite the unlikelihood of such, they both came to believe in later years that they started to fall in love that evening. The rest of the summer strengthened that feeling. There were more square dances, and softball games and cookouts and hikes together, and more kissing. Linda, then 17, made a determined effort to keep Martha Stevens, still on the scene, successfully at a distance.

The first time she met Chris, a nervous college freshman coming to pick up his date for a movie and meeting her mother for the first time, Marn impulsively asked him to dance. Imagine his shock! Chris came from a rather formal, austere family, and he had never been asked to dance by anyone that he could recall. There is no information in the family memory banks as to whether or not he actually did dance with her, but he remembers very clearly wanting to get the hell out of there as fast as possible. Turns out, she was suspicious of this college man who had stolen her oldest daughter's heart, so she thought she'd stir things up a bit and see how he handled it. I'm guessing she was not overly impressed.

It seems Ted Robinson made an effort to check out his daughter's suitor as well. Chris was a member of the ROTC at Yale, and he had word one day that an Air Force officer by the name of Col. Robinson was coming to interview him. Chris knew instantly who this was, and he was quite certain that Col. Robinson knew the score too. But there was not even a hint of their connection during the interview.

In high school, Linda excelled in almost every subject. At some point, she is said to have been given an IQ test, on which she scored as a genius. She applied to several colleges and was accepted to many. Her first choice was Middlebury College, as it offered a field of study for those considering a diplomatic career, which interested her, but she eventually chose Connecticut College, where she was given a full scholarship, and could live in a cooperative dorm called Emily Abbey House. Her decision most likely had more to do with Chris being at Yale than anything, as the two colleges are very close to one another.

It was tough on the others when Linda left – Polly especially. Linnie had been like a second mother to Polly. Susan was on the school basketball and field hockey teams, and she managed the softball team, so Polly was left to her own devices a lot. She always looked forward to Thursday afternoons, when she and Sue sang alto together in the Glee Club at school. Both of them had so much singing and harmonizing practice at home with Marn that they were chosen to go to Symphony Hall in Boston to be in an all-state chorus performance. All the students learned their parts at their home schools, and then sang together in Boston. Marn could not have been more proud, and went along as a chaperone (her only way to get to the performance).

Having only two daughters at home cut a little from the food bill, but Marn's little family was not out of the woods yet. They still struggled to make ends meet. One winter day Polly and Susan, ages 15 and 17 mind you, were entrusted with the last twenty dollars Marn had for the week to go to Collins

Market – right across the street – and buy some food. They had a list and brought a sled along to pull the bundles home. When they arrived at the check-out counter, they couldn't find the money, and so charged it to Marn's account. Back at home, their faces fell as Marn explained that she had no money to pay the tab. It was yet another lesson in surviving tough times. The girls began getting jobs babysitting (often taking care of the Bandolin children next door, who adored the Robinson girls), and always gave their earnings to Marn. The family opened up a savings account at the bank, and were finally able to buy their first car a couple of years later.

What an exciting day that was! One of the gals at the phone company was married to a used car salesman, who picked out a Pontiac Catalina 2-door sedan for them. Only a few years old, and a pretty turquoise color. Mr. Statler gave them quite a deal on the car as Midge was such a good friend of his wife's, and he always serviced the car personally. He delivered it to the house on a Saturday morning, honking the horn unnecessarily, as all the Robinsons were already standing on the front steps. Polly and Susan clapped and jumped up and down, and Marnie beamed with pride. Mr. Statler held the driver's side door open for Marn, to whom it hadn't occurred that she would have to learn how to drive it. He showed her the gas and brake pedals, the turn indicator and shift levers, laughing at her casual way.

As the girls approached, however, she waved them off, suggesting that maybe they should wait until she'd been around the block a few times. But Mr. Statler laughed and waved them forward, so they climbed into the back and went sailing off down the road, with Midge Robinson at the wheel. She took to it like a champ, driving down Old Sudbury Road as though she'd been doing this for years. It was a

Polly and Susan

level of freedom the family had never known, and a real validation for Marnie. She had arrived at a new level of comfort, status and accomplishment.

Some people worry when things are looking up; they wonder what is around the next corner. Not our Marn. She relished the good times, rolling along as though they would never end. So she was not prepared when, just a short few months later, the phone company went to a dial system. It represented progress for the town of Wayland, but of course it meant there was no longer a need for so many operators, and Marn lost her job. This was devastating for her; there were very few jobs an unskilled lady could hold in a small town like Wayland. And she could not go back to her sister Sissy for another loan. She began to have bad dreams of being even more destitute than her little family had ever been.

Even though she was heading into the depths of yet another downturn in her luck, she rallied her energy, making sure birthdays that year were observed with special fanfare. There was never much in the way of presents, but it was always a very special day, and the birthday girl was made to feel like a princess. And there was cake. That year, Polly remembers getting a sweater that she swears was a hand-me-down and a book that might have already been in the house but just wrapped up for the occasion. And yet, when they sat at the dinner table, and Marn told Polly how special she was – how lucky Marn felt to be her mother, despite the many grey hairs she had gotten from raising her — Polly remembers feeling absolutely blessed. Polly may have been a brat, but she was really not a spoiled brat.

Our brave Midge went through many a sleepless night, trying to figure out what to do, as the months went by, to keep the roof over their heads, while trying also to keep things cheery. She broke down only once that anyone can remember, on that Christmas morning. Linda was home from college, and it was tradition that the girls were not to come down until Marn turned on the hi-fi. Although they were a little old for such a game, the three of them waited obediently at the top of the stairs. As they lounged on the steps, they heard Marn begin to weep. The three teens ran down the stairs, nighties flying, to find Marn sitting with her face in her hands in front of the Christmas tree. They tried to comfort her, telling her that all they cared about was being together – they figured she was feeling guilty about the dearth of gifts under the tree. Finally, she blurted out that the hi-fi was broken, and how was she supposed to come up with the money for that? The girls folded her into a big flannel hug, making her sobbing turn into more of a wail, which after a while made the girls start to snicker, and eventually the whole thing turned into a wonderful Christmas.

Shortly into the new year, as luck would have it, a professional man — a dentist — moved his office to town. Midge applied for and was given a job as his receptionist. The office was in a white house next to the train station in the center of Wayland – on the right, you will see a little illustration of the Wayland Train Station, with Dr. Chamberlin's office behind it. It was actually two houses, that were connected by a long hallway. The house in back was rented out to tenants. And in front, on the second floor above the office, there was a little apartment that

Home for the
Holidays

Marn was offered — they could live there for free. What a stroke of luck! The apartment was really just two bedrooms – three if you counted the tiny room under the eaves — and a half bath. If the Robinson girls wanted to have a bath, they had to go downstairs before office hours began and use the bathroom off the waiting room, and they were forever getting caught, running through the waiting room in their bathrobes (Just one bathrobe actually – like so many other things, they shared this). Still, it was free.

This was a wonderful job for Marn, so outgoing was she and so responsible. Her phone manners were impeccable of course, but the best part of the job was her new boss, Dr. Chamberlin. If there was ever anyone who could match her toe-to-toe for fun, it was he. The office took on the amusing personality of these two, and even the patients began to look forward to going for their dental check-ups. And when, a year or so into the job, Dr. Chamberlin needed a new dental assistant, Marnie got promoted to the position, assisting him in extractions and root canals – despite the fact that she had no training whatsoever. They would sing and talk over their patients

– I'm sure they calmed more than a few nervous nerves with their zany banter.

So the little family settled into their new digs. Marn loved being able to see more of Polly and Susan, working right downstairs as she did, but she was very strict about them staying out of the office. Unless there was a dire emergency, they were to steer clear. Once office hours ended, at 5:00 on the dot, they were permitted to use the waiting room as their living room and cook their meals in the little office kitchen.

In her senior year of high school, Susan was part of the Speech Club and was invited to go to the semi-finals at Colby College in Maine to compete. It would have been a real hardship to get her up there, but in a wonderful show of human kindness, one of her teachers drove her up and back that weekend. Susan didn't win anything, but had the time of her life, and returned the next fall on a partial scholarship, traveling all by herself on the train to Waterville and finding the campus once the train pulled in to the station. There was a little extra money in the till at this point, as they were living rent-free, and it was applied to Susan's tuition.

Before school began, Marnie took Polly and Susan on a madcap weekend on Cape Cod. She had somehow arranged for them to stay at a seaside cottage, and they ate clams and walked the beach and communed with the natives. It was a nice send-off for Sue, and ended up becoming a tradition for the three of them a few years hence.

Polly, Midge and Susan

So now our Midge was down two daughters, having only Paulina still at home, finishing up her senior year of high school. The two of them made a comic duet, now that the two more serious members of the family had flown the coop. It was particularly nice, she always said, to be finally able to get her youngest daughter all to herself. They discovered a kinship that year which bonded them in a special way for the rest of Marn's life.

Meanwhile, Chris Harris kept courting Linda, although Polly was adamantly opposed to Linda falling in love with anybody, as that would mean she'd have to get married and leave the family. So she would do things like parade around the house in her underwear when he came to call at holidays, or hang from the tree by the front door to scare him when he approached. That he continued to come around said a lot about how much he loved Linda, so many roadblocks and tests were thrown his way.

Sadly, Susan was asked to leave Colby after that year, by Marnie herself. Never one to complain, Susan nevertheless carried a little grudge about this for the rest of her life, as the reason she was given was that they needed the money to send Polly to Walnut Hill, a private school in Natick. My suspicion, with all due respect, is that Susan flunked out of Colby, or Marn never would have taken her out. If she had been scoring well in her classes, I think Marn would have done anything in her power to keep her there. Of course, there may have been some very compelling reason why Polly needed to get out of the public school – with her reputation as a troublemaker, she may have been marked by either the faculty or the students… or both. Anyway, Susan ended up at The Chandler School in Boston, where she could live at home. She got a two-year degree in accounting, which suited her very well and stood her in good stead for the rest of her working life. She got herself a job at Raytheon, an electronics company with an office located in Wayland, where she met the man she would later marry, a kind of whiz-bang engineer named Tom Shepard.

Tom seemed to be a deep, thoughtful guy, so it was quite a surprise to Susan when, for their first date, he took her to a strip club. He sat with his back to the stage and seemed to have no interest in what was going on up there. And Susan had foregone her glasses for the evening (Because, as we all know, men don't make passes at girls who wear glasses), so she was spared the details as well.

Susan, in her glasses

Shortly after he and Susan began dating, Tom came by the office one evening to say he'd set up a blind date for Polly. Polly hated blind dates. "Is he tall, at least?" she begged. If there was one thing worse than a blind date, it was a short blind date. Tom assured her that he was tall enough and a very nice guy.

Polly and Susan were upstairs getting dressed for their double-date when Tom and his friend arrived that Saturday night. Polly had picked out the basics of her outfit for the evening, but since she didn't know exactly how tall he was – Polly was pretty tall herself – she was waiting to be told whether she should wear heels or flats. In those days, it was a real faux pas to be taller than your date, so this was always a consideration for tall gals.

Marn came to the foot of the stairs and called softly up to Polly, who peeked out from around her bedroom door.

"Well?" she asked.

Marn hesitated for a moment as she thought of how to say it. "How about," she suggested, "you just chop yourself off at the knees?"

Tom Shepard turned out to be quite the alcoholic, and Marn was none too thrilled at her daughter's choice. He was also older and divorced, with three children from his first wife. But Susan fell in love with him, and, in a rare show of willfulness, she defied Marn by marrying him. But I'm getting ahead of myself here.

When it was Polly's turn to think about college, she was enrolled at Mt. Ida College in Newton. This was a neat trick on Marn's part. She was all out of money for college, but she could claim that Polly was handicapped because of her club foot, and so Polly got into college for free on some sort of government handout program. Polly was horrified to be classified as handicapped, but at least she got to go to college. She wanted to major in English, but her grades were not deemed to be acceptable by the dean of the department. Her high school grades were pretty horrid, to tell you the truth. She had an advisor who really took to her, though, noticing in her a special spark. He suggested, given her outgoing personality, that she study retailing, and she was somehow able to squeak through the program to graduation. (It may have been a two-year program, which seems more do-able for someone like our Polly who lacked the patience and attitude for serious study.)

Once she was done with school, her retailing degree in hand, Polly began to make plans to look for work around Wayland, so she could move back home. Marn had other ideas, however. She was probably more than ready to get Polly out of the house! So Marn and Linda hatched a little plan to get her to move to New York, a matter in which Polly seemingly had little choice. She would share an apartment with Linda's old pal Susan Colliton, who was now living in the city, and find a way to earn money.

"But Mom," whined Polly, "How am I going to get a job?"

"You just got a retailing degree! You march yourself up and down Fifth Avenue," answered Marn authoritatively, "and go to the Personnel Departments in the stores. You'll get a job."

Polly tried this for a day, and called Marn to tell her every last detail of how unsuccessful she had been. "And you won't believe it!" she said, "There are Negroes just walking around everywhere!"

Well, I wasn't there, and neither were you, so we have to imagine the tongue-lashing Polly received for this comment. Marn was aghast at how truly naïve her daughter was. One wonders how Marn was enlightened enough to understood that it was wrong to say things like that, having lived her whole life in communities almost completely devoid of people of color. Surely, no one had ever taken the time to teach her about tolerance as a child – she was always less than reverent when it came to her religious upbringing, and the only other possibility would have been Aunt Mary and Aunt Rose, who don't seem to have taught her anything. So it must have come by her naturally; it appears she never had any racial prejudice.

"Tomorrow is another day," she said finally, "Try again – and be sure and be polite to anyone you meet. Do you hear me? Anyone, Polly."

Embarrassed, Polly hung out the phone. The next morning, she set out again, and again the day after that, and eventually got a job at Bonwit Teller on Fifth Avenue, a famed upscale department store specializing in high-end women's apparel. She was hired at $48 per week in the glove department. It was at Bonwit's that she met co-workers Mary Smith and Merle Iseli, both of them young Europeans — and the three of them had a ball in the city, going to parties, eating at cheap dives, giggling and screaming and having wild times. Merle, Mary and Polly remained close friends for the rest of their lives.

If it was hard for Marn to see her girls leave the nest, she had a little something else on her mind, which may have eased the pain. At some point along the way her boss, Dr. Chamberlin, became Hal, and it was not long before the two had a little thing going. The family joke is that she started answering the phones, moved up to assistant, and then moved up again to sleeping with the boss, but I have no doubt that the two truly loved each other. The trouble – a problem she had encountered before – was that Hal was married. In his case however, his marriage was already on shaky ground. (Bill Edwards, by the way, never left his wife Alice. In fact, both of them remained family friends, Alice none the wiser)

At the same time, undaunted and despite Polly's efforts to horrify him, Chris continued to woo Linda, eventually winning her hand in marriage. Linda dropped out of college and married Chris on October 8, 1955 at the Martha Mary Chapel on the grounds of the historic Wayside Inn in Sudbury.

The spring before they married, Ted Robinson paid a visit to Linda at Connecticut College, to make yet another one of his offers. He showed up in his starched dress uniform, took her (and Polly, who had arranged to be visiting when she got wind of his invitation) out to lunch, and offered to pay for the entire wedding if she would allow him to walk her down the aisle.

She turned him down flat.

Linda was old enough to remember the events surrounding his departure from their family those many years before, and her allegiance was with her mother all the way. She would never have allowed him to be a part of her wedding, even if it meant a fancy party, because it would have been too much for Marn to bear. And, she said, she couldn't stand the thought of him giving her hand to Chris in marriage, when he'd never been there for her. "I'm not his to give away," she boldly stated.

But because Linda, and later Polly, were marrying into families of decidedly higher economic status than the Robinsons, there was some behind-the-scenes fussing, to try, if not to impress them, at least show them that the family had roots, education, manners and class. Sissy and Bill Bartel threw an engagement party for the couple at their home in Weston. Marn's brother Jack was behind the bar, and Polly and Susan passed hors d'oeuvres. This was a rather grand gesture on the Bartels' part — considering they were so on the outs with Marn — but that doesn't equate to it being a great party. Photos of the event don't make it look like much fun. Linda's future in-laws appear clustered and looking a little grim, with the exception of one picture of Chris' stepmother, who looks like she is singing with Hal Chamberlin. Surely she was not. The party was probably not a great impression-maker, but it was also probably a better bet than the boisterous singing and drinking bash that the Robinsons would have put on. These were not two families who would ever mix well.

Staid though it was, the one notable moment of this particular evening was the arrival of Midge's sister Nana. She had run through three husbands at this point, including the most recent to a jazz musician who had run off into the night, and everyone in the family was worried about Nana's behavior, known, as she was, for being quite a lush. They would all have been thrilled to see her except for the circumstances; she could easily bring the whole evening to a crescendo by making a drunken fool of herself in front of everyone.

Sure enough, as she entered the living room from the hall, she did not notice that there was a step down, which she missed, falling on her face into the assembled guests. The family gasped collectively, thinking it was just typical Nana, drunk again, embarrassing everybody.

The fact was that she hadn't had a drink in two days (no mean feat for her) in order to avoid embarrassing them. And she managed to get through the entire affair cold sober. It was a powerful testament to her love for her sister and her niece Linnie, and it showed the best side of Nana.

When she took Nana back to her hotel that night, Marnie surreptitiously smuggled out with her a mayonnaise jar filled with .gin. As they said their goodnights, Marn held out the jar. You never saw a more grateful face! But as Nana reached for it, it slipped from her hand and smashed on the ground. Marn offered to go back to the house,

Midge, Nana and Sissy

some 20 minutes away by car, to get some more gin, but Nana spared her, and they said their goodnights.

That fall, Linda's wedding went off with classic Marnie ingenuity; that is to say it was lovely but how did she ever pay for it? Chris flew in from Chicago, where he had just landed a new job, two days before the wedding. Linda was beside herself with excitement, walking on her tiptoes around the house for days before. Her spirits flared up in anger momentarily toward her new father-in-law when he wouldn't bring her to meet Chris at Logan Airport, but except for that she was on cloud nine, so in love with him was she.

It was a grand affair. Chris' parents hosted a bridal dinner at the Union Club (a very up-scale and starchy old institution in Boston), and the wedding was a colossal climactic event for everyone, at least everyone in Marn's family. The fact that it was a rainy day did not dampen any spirits. Linda wore her mother's wedding dress, and someone came up with

Chris and Linda

a big, ancient — but fancy — black Buick, in which Chris' brother Larry drove them from the chapel to the reception at the Wayside Inn (which was all of about 200 feet away). Marnie must have been in hock up to her eyeballs from the expense of it all.

That night, after the wedding reception, Marn was driven home by Linda's friend and bridesmaid Sandy Maxwell and her boyfriend Tom, along with Polly. Marn passed out on the sofa in the office waiting room, clearly exhausted from all the excitement. Plus she was drunk as a skunk. When it was time for bed, Sandy was loath to leave Marn (and Tom, also smashed and passed out) sprawled downstairs. She talked Polly into helping her get the two of them upstairs. And so they somehow managed to get the two revelers up from their couches, and practically dragged them to the stairs. As they were struggling up the narrow staircase, Sandy looked at Polly and said, "Isn't this fun?!" Polly, who had managed drunken people on a few previous occasions in her life and had never thought of it as fun before, had to agree, and the two of them giggled and screamed their way up to the second floor. They tucked Marn into her bed, and deposited Tom on the daybed in the tiny room under the eaves with all the wedding gifts (they could only clear a small spot for him on the bed, so he woke the next morning surrounded by silver and china).

Chris and Linda moved to Illinois for his new job with Rand McNally right after their honeymoon in their beloved Randolph, and I was born a year and change later. Marnie suffered mightily to have her first-born taken so far away, and for Linda Robinson (now Linda Harris) to go through pregnancy and the birth of her first child without her mother nearby must have seemed very unnatural to both women. Marn did find a way to come out for a visit to meet me in my first few months of life, and it wasn't long before my family moved back east, to Great Neck, a suburb of New York City, where my brother Stephen was born.

Back home in Wayland, meanwhile, Marn had put her foot down, asking Hal in no uncertain terms to make up his mind about marrying her; to shit or get off the pot, as we say in this family. When he hemmed and hawed (or whatever he did besides say yes immediately), she left for New York herself, moving in with her old pals Rosie and Todd, who lived near us in Port Washington. She got herself a job, with remarkable speed, in the city at Lord & Taylor – the woman knew how to talk her way into a job.

Rose and Todd had a little daughter named Cindy at that point, and in a recent conversation, Cindy Kenney spoke of the wonderful times when Marn lived with them. She remembered being called "pink bug" by Marn (more later about my nickname and everyone else's). She remembered laughter and singing and feeling so special in Marn's eyes, and I know Rose and Todd helped Marn to sort things out, great friends that they were to her.

So for that period, Marn lived near Linda, which was wonderful for them. And with Polly in New York City, they were both regular visitors at our apartment, and there were many high times during that period. In fact, somewhere in there, Susan left Tom too, when she thought a proposal ought to be forthcoming. Or maybe it was that she just wanted to be with everyone else…. She went to live with Polly in the city, so for a short while all three daughters, and Marn, lived in very close proximity. Polly and Susan would often take the train out to Great Neck on Friday night and spend the weekend at our apartment, and the three sisters would go shopping or out to lunch on Saturday, with me and my brother in tow, or they would go and visit Marn at Rose and Todd's, where all hilarity would break loose.

Polly, Linda and Susan with Kim in foreground

It was around this time that Marn's daughters got the idea to send her on a cruise. They all pitched in on it, and Marn was secretly horrified. Going off by herself was the last thing she wanted to do, but she went along with it. She did end up having a ball, but I remember the send-off party – in those days, everyone came on board to see someone off on a cruise, drinking champagne in the traveler's stateroom, which would normally be cause for a jolly party, but this was more a case of convincing Marn that she'd have fun.

After the cruise, Marn returned to Massachusetts, but not into the apartment over Hal's office. She moved into a modest apartment on a small farm in nearby Sudbury. Susan had returned to Boston, where she and Marn began to bicker over Tom. Marnie really didn't approve of him, and had secretly been hoping that their separation would quell any further developments. But Susan was in love, and she fought for her rights.

She had help from none other than Tom himself, who was not about to let Susan's mother tell him what he could and could not do. He took to declaring his love for her by camping out on the front lawn of their house, hanging his clothes in the bushes and sleeping in a pile of blankets in the grass. He is rumored to have told Marn during an exchange that she could "go shit in her hat" if she thought she could stop them. They married in 1960, also at the Martha Mary Chapel.

And so Tom came into the family, who gradually found that, while he was a drunk, he was a very lovable one. Certainly, someone who drank was going to fit in better than someone who didn't! He eventually found AA, became sober, and went on to inspire and help countless others who were struggling with alcohol — at the ceremony following his death, dozens of strangers showed up, telling the assembled group about how Tom had saved their lives, showed them the path out of alcoholism, and held their hand along the way. One couple had named their baby after him.

But for a while there, he was a rip-roaring drunk. He didn't remember anything about their wedding, for example, being already bombed when he stood in the church for their ceremony.

Linda, Tom and Susan

At some point, Tom quit his big job at the electronics firm to become a carpenter and a potter, and Susan mostly supported the family on her earnings as a bookkeeper. She seemed quite happy to do that, so great was her love for Tom and their children, but it is also true that Susan rarely complained or said no to anything. When Tom died – at a fairly young age from prostate cancer — Sue went through an agony like I've never seen. She seemed to have lost her compass. We had a birthday party for her a week or so after Tom's death, and she cried softly the whole time she was opening her presents and eating her birthday cake.

But back to our story. It was not long after Sue and Tom's wedding that Hal divorced his wife, and he and Marn picked up where they had left off. He had gained quite a bit of respect for her, and I think the fact that she was so adamant about him divorcing – when she had seemed to have no qualms about sleeping with a married man or two in the past – shows that she thought he was pretty special too.

It was also not long after Susan got married that Polly met her future husband too. She had gone along with a friend or two to a house party in a very tony New York neighborhood. Once they'd made it into the throng, Polly announced, to no one in particular, that she needed a drink. A handsome young man standing nearby offered to get her one. This was the man she would one day marry, Palmer Sealy, Jr., who was there with a date. But as the evening wore on, he couldn't help noticing how fun Polly was, how real. At some point he asked for her telephone number and, as he was leaving the party, he called over his date's shoulder to Polly, reciting her number to her from memory. He called the next day, and when Susan told Polly that there was a guy named Palmer on the phone (Apparently, she hadn't gotten his name the night before), she replied that it was the stupidest name she'd ever heard. She claims not to have been terribly impressed with him, which is rather an irony, as theirs was to be a storybook tale of love and family. Palmer went on to become wealthy in the New York commercial real estate business, and was the consummate good guy. An ardent adherent to old world manners, he raised his three boys to be gentlemen just by setting a good example. And he loved our Polly like nobody's business, handful that she was.

Polly's wedding, like the weddings of all the Robinson girls, was an event

to be remembered. There were high spirits and
happiness to be had by the boatload, with
dancing and singing and cake, and with pretty
bridesmaids and men in tuxedoes. Hal
Chamberlin walked Polly down the aisle, and
Marn did all she could to make it nice, just as she
had done for the others. They had all worn the
same wedding dress, and corners were cut
wherever possible. But when preparing for
Polly's wedding, which was to be held in the side

*From left to right: Marnie,
Sissy's daughter Anne, Polly, Susan,
Linda's son Stephen and Nana.*

yard of the farm in Sudbury where Marn lived, the bride-to-be had a little
tantrum over their chipped cups and mismatched serving plates – they could
not afford to rent anything beyond a tent, and so were using their own china.
"Polly," Marn said with authority, in a phrase that was to be remembered
long after it was uttered, "We are what we are."

Beyond the expense, it is to Marn's credit that she did as much as she did,
as she probably did not approve of any of her daughters' suitors. Still, she
never intervened in relationships. It was her view that parents can teach their
children things until the age of about 16. Beyond that, there's no point, she'd
say. By the time they start listening again, they are all grown up anyway, in
spite of you. So the three girls, once they achieved the age of sweet sixteen,
were more or less allowed to explore the world with her blessing, secure in
the knowledge that she was there for them always.

All three of her daughters married young and stayed married until death
parted them. So how is it that we all say that Marnie, with her colorful history,

was a good example? That she taught us everything we needed to know in this arena? The answer is that what she taught us was not about relationships. It had nothing to do with relationships. It was about love and family. And on that subject, she was the expert.

Polly on the way to her honeymoon.

Once Marn had all of her girls out of the house, she was free to do as she pleased, at least more so than when she had to provide them with a home. Surely, the freedom also allowed her to engage in romantic pursuits with Hal, as their relationship grew, and she was able to enjoy the fruits of her labors of raising her daughters and getting them successfully married off. She must have been so pleased to see them happy, especially considering the bad example she felt she had set. Even though Ted had been the one to cheat on her, impregnate someone else, and then dump her, Marn always told her girls that it took two to make a divorce. I don't think she really elaborated on that statement, but it was one of her many mantras.

Linda's family moved to Connecticut in 1961, which meant a longer trip for Polly to come and spend time with her big sister. Plus now she had to drag her husband with her, and Palmer was not crazy about this arrangement. He had worked all week, and thought he was entitled to some relaxation at the weekend. Also, he and Linda's husband Chris differed strongly when it came to politics, and neither of them could seem to avoid bringing it up. But he went along with it because Polly simply could not be apart from her family and he knew it.

It was also a long trip from Connecticut to go and see Marn, but my family went often. The accommodations at the LeBlanc farm in Sudbury allowed for her to have room for us to stay when we came to visit. What fun it was to visit her there! She had gotten herself a dog, her wonderful Collie Taffy, and there were sheep and cows and chickens and a pond into which my brother fell once and was rescued by the brave Taffy. There was a little brook where we could catch turtles and frogs and a lovely hammock between two towering Maple trees. Polly's wedding reception was held on the expansive lawn there.

I think those were happy years for Marn, and after a few years, Hal proposed marriage and she accepted. He arranged for them to move into the house that was attached to his dental office, which had been rented to tenants previously. The two had a little wedding ceremony in 1965, just for family, and she left the farm and moved in with him. They ceremoniously planted a pine tree in the back yard that they called the Loving Tree. Every year the tree grew and grew, and it was a marriage that would last for the rest of Marn's life.

I can scarcely imagine what it must have been like for Marn to find Hal. After virtually a lifetime of struggle, she found a mate who showered her with affection, who paid the household bills, and who provided a buddy to go through life with — It must have been such a weight off her shoulders!

I can't recall this topic ever being brought up in family prattles, the discussions that happen virtually every time two or more of Marnie's family members are together for more than a few hours, in which updates and family scuttlebutt are shared, and – invariably – an old story is remembered. No, I have come upon this myself: She finally had someone to take care of her.

And take care of her he did. He took care of all of us, walking Polly down the aisle at her wedding, taking Sue and Tom in when their house burned down, and doing the same for me and my brother and sister when our mom died. But the way he took care of Marn was special. He made life fun, just as she had always done for all of us. Together, they went off in search of high adventure, always having a grand time. The two of them went traipsing off to Martha's Vineyard, Cape Cod or Bermuda, coming home with sunburned noses and stories to tell of all the adventures they'd had and the people they'd met. They loved eating in local dives, spending time on beaches or poolside, and soaking up the native color. Sometimes they went by cruise ship, but they also traveled in Hal's Volkswagen camper. As a kid, that camper fascinated me; it had all the amenities of home – even running water – in a car!

Midge and the camper

They would pull up to a campground, beach or wherever, fling open the doors, and start having fun. I can remember that camper festooned with wet bathing suits when we were near water, turning out meals at dinnertime, and providing a backdrop for so many memorable moments.

Wherever they found themselves, a party or adventure was likely to ensue. Rain or shine, on land or sea, with paper cups or fine crystal (more often paper cups), the two of them just caused the best kind of fun to break out.

Marn's daughters inherited her love of fun, and they instilled it in their kids in turn. Family gatherings were, and continue to be, hilarious and wildly fun. I have early memories of family softball games in which all the adults played, including Marnie – she had a mean leftie swing. There were martinis at every base, so the games got sillier and sillier as the innings passed, with people crashing into each other trying to catch the ball, and the rules getting modified constantly. It was a fabulous era.

Tom and baby Tim

A bunch of new grandchildren came along after Marn and Hal were married. Polly gave birth to Palmer III, known as Chip, and then David. She had been, as she said, "knocked out" for Chip's birth, but had Dave by natural childbirth, which she loved so much that she got pregnant again right away and had Jeff. But not before Susan had given birth to Tim. Then my mom had Annie, almost ten years my junior. So now there were seven grandchildren, and all of them felt they were Marn's favorite. We each had our own nickname; I was Angel Puff, Steve was Lovey Boy, and my sister was Fluffhead. And Marn had so much love that no one ever felt slighted. We were each of us treasured.

PART FOUR

Just as things were going so well for Midge, tragedy befell her again. It was in October of 1967 that Linda died, at just 31 years of age.

My mother's death was like to have killed Marn.

I was a few months shy of 11 years old, my brother Steve had just turned nine, and little Annie was at about 18 months. As for my father, he was as happy as he ever would be – something in him died when Linda died. But he was happy then. He has always been into photo-documenting things, and there is a photo that was taken a few short days before she died – Dad had set up the camera on a timer and then run into the photo. There we all are, looking happy, well adjusted, content. Stephen has a look of utter self-confidence, and Chris, my dad, is gazing lovingly at us all. (I think I look like a young Italian starlet, but that's not really germane.) And Linda? Let's talk about Linda a little.

My mother was a very special person, pure and simple. Warm and smart, tender and so caring. Sainted though she has become in the family, I know this is true because I was there, for the ten years or so of my life before she died. My little brother remembers much less, my sister nothing. And Linda was a yummy mommy. She had loads of experience, having so often played the mother role for her sisters, so I think she was more comfortable with it than your average young mom. But she also retained that love of fun – perhaps not as much as her sisters, owing to the calm seriousness of her nature, but I can remember her getting down on the floor with us as though she were another youngster, delighting in childish play.

Linda played the guitar and sang the folk songs that Joan Baez was making popular at that time. She was an ardent Democrat, volunteering with the League of Women Voters and Lyndon Johnson's presidential campaign – some of my earliest memories are of playing on the floor at Democratic Headquarters – and she was widely respected for her intelligence among her little group of friends, all much older than she. We sang in the car a lot, and she took us on jaunts to the city to meet Dad for lunch, or to a museum or the zoo or a hike in the woods. But when I think of my mom, it is almost always of her sunshiny smile, which she lavished on her children almost as though she knew she might not always be there.

When I was ten, our family moved for a year to Switzerland on something of a lark, my father thinking it would be enriching for his children to experience living in a foreign country. And so he got a special assignment to spend a year working for a Swiss company, renting our house in Connecticut to another family for the year we'd be gone, and made arrangements for the family to travel by ocean liner to Europe. We would land in Rotterdam, where a brand-new Volkswagen mini-bus would be waiting for us upon disembarking.

From there, the family spent the summer traveling at a leisurely pace, passing through Holland and Germany on the way to our destination in Lausanne. It was a marvelous adventure; we stayed in a fancy hotel in Amsterdam and a 16th century castle in Germany – it was heaven for two spunky American kids like my younger brother and me, and, I think, very romantic for my parents. Once we arrived in Lausanne, I quickly picked up the language, and was allowed occasionally to go with Steve to the shops down the street, where we bought the croissants and baguettes our family enjoyed at lunch on the sunny terrace behind the villa we had rented for the year. I kept in touch with my friends from the states, sending postcards from all the exciting places we visited, telling them about the fun of riding around Lake Geneva in a pedal boat, going to a glacier in the middle of summer, and exploring old castle ruins. We planned to travel to the charming village of Zermatt for the Christmas holiday, a plan that never came to be as Mom died just after Stephen's birthday that fall.

Dear reader, I could write a whole book about Linda dying. It was a beautiful crisp autumn day, and Steve and I came home from goofing around along the sidewalks down the hill from our villa. Mom was cooking supper at the stove when she complained of light-headedness. She sat on a chair for a moment, eventually being helped to a sofa by her cousin Anne (Sissy's daughter), who was staying with us. (Imagine if Anne had not been there! We had no way to contact our father, who was off at his job.) Anyway, it was very quick – she lay down on the sofa, closed her eyes, and died.

That is the very much-abbreviated version of one of the most pivotal events of this writer's life, but it serves its purpose until the next book.

On the night Linda died, Chris sat down at the ancient phone table in the front hallway of our Swiss villa and placed a call to Wayland, Massachusetts, to Marnie and Hal's house on Old Sudbury Road. Dad had the awful task of telling Marn that her precious daughter was gone. He asked Hal, who answered the phone, to hold her very tight, and he delivered his terrible news, that Linda had died. Through his shock and tears, Hal asked very few questions, mostly only saying that he and Marn would catch the first plane they could to meet the family in Switzerland. "Hal," my father asked, "what is that noise I hear in the background?" "It's Marjorie," Hal answered. Marnie was keening – a strange, animal-like sound that, once you've heard it, you never forget it. A vocal lament as sad and unearthly as could be, seemingly specific to the Irish. Susan did the same thing years later, when her beloved Tom died.

Marnie keened into the night, wailing and sobbing and railing at God. She declared the next morning that there was no God. No god would take her Linda, so young and sweet, the mother of her first-born grandchildren. Of all the hardships my grandmother had endured – and, as you know, there had been plenty of them – this may have been the hardest one.

Marnie and Hal arrived in Switzerland late the next day – as we drove to the airport to pick them up, the sun broke through the clouds, sending brilliant rays streaming down from the heavens to the earth. Perhaps, my father suggested very uncharacteristically, it was a message to us from Mom.

Hal and Marn helped us to pack, and Steve and I were withdrawn from the international school we had attended. How well I remember the sad faces of the other students when I went into my classroom to say goodbye. We had only just met a month earlier when school began, but they all seemed genuinely to feel my pain. I received a card from them, my class at Ecole Nouvelle, a month or so after we got back to the U.S., with messages from each of them; mostly in English but some in French or German.

Steve and I went into Lausanne with Hal that afternoon (I imagine it was a way to get us out of the house for a while), and found ourselves giggling together as Hal tried to speak French to the shopkeepers. To us, he was the nuttiest guy, and I remember it being lots of fun; we had to rescue him more than once, as our French was much better than his, and he was using the wrong words (perhaps deliberately) to our great delight. It is hard to imagine that any of us could have even smiled that day, and yet here I was, having a ball and showing off my confident proficiency with the language.

I know now that the healing had begun, on that silly day in the streets of a European city.

It wasn't until years later that I knew how close I came to a very different reality in the year after Mom's death. We couldn't move back to Connecticut as we had rented out the house there for the year. And my father's parents naturally assumed that we would move in with them, at their immaculate country house located outside Concord, Mass. They had gone so far as to enroll me in Concord Academy and Steve at Middlesex, both prestigious private schools nearby. But in a courageous move, Dad announced that we would live instead with Marnie in Wayland. Undoubtedly this came as a surprise to his parents, but it was oh, so the right thing to do. And so we moved into Old Sudbury Road, living in the same small rooms and half-bathroom over Hal's dental practice office where Marn and her daughters had lived so many years before. We were enrolled in the local elementary school – I remember my Dad waiting with us for the school bus on that first day at our new school, lightening our anxiety by telling us that he had panicked, momentarily, until he realized he did not have to communicate with the bus driver in French. Dad was reinstated at his old job in New York, so he was away a lot, often staying with Polly and Palmer in Forest Hills.

Next came Thanksgiving, a big family affair, and I remember feeling so warmed by this loving, noisy, fun group. But it is Christmas that stands out. For the days and weeks before, we had secrets, baked cookies and decorated the tree – complete with the candle ornaments that bubble when they are lit

The night that the Christmas tree was first standing in the living room, I sat, all by my ten-year-old self, in the darkening evening, with only the twinkling lights on the tree to light the room. I let my vision go in and out of focus as I gazed at our tree. I hugged myself and thought of my mother. I wished very hard for a miracle. I knew it was a wish that could not come true, but still I wished it. Marnie came into the room and, seeming to know what I was thinking, sat by my side and wrapped her arms around me. She kissed my head and combed her fingers through my hair. "My angel," she whispered. We sat for a moment together, looking up at the splendor of the tree before us. "I miss Mom," I whispered to her, barely able to even get the words out before I broke down and sobbed into her shoulder. "Oh, sweetie, of course you do…that's right, you cry." she cooed. I let all my sadness flow into her, as she held me and made soothing sounds. It was like a great dam giving way. I opened my eyes at one point to see Steve and Harold standing at the door to the kitchen. They looked so worried for me but quickly whisked themselves away from my private moment with Marn and my sadness.

My sobs subsided slowly, and when at last I was calm, she took me by my shoulders and looked into my eyes. She told me how much my mother had loved me. "She was so proud of you," she said, her words a salve on my wounded soul. She told me how pretty I was, and how smart, and what a good big sister. Her words were similar to Mom's, but different also. Unconditional love it was, but not that of a mother. There was a seriousness; she wanted me to hear and understand her words. She was not so much mothering me as teaching me. Marnie did a lot of teaching. That night, in front of our glittering Christmas tree, I knew I should always try to listen closely to what she said.

Christmas Eve arrived, and there was much flurry. Hal had lots of holiday traditions – reading The Night before Christmas as we hung the stockings –

all ten of them! He lit the little candle-tree on the mantle, roasted chestnuts on the fire and made those special almonds. And late in the afternoon, Hal began making taffy. He and his eldest son Tommy, home for the holiday from Middlebury College, threw the taffy onto a hook on the back of the kitchen door, stretching it again and again. It took a great deal of strength, and I marveled at the two men stripped to their undershirts, their foreheads shining with sweat. When the taffy had been stretched to their satisfaction, they pulled it into long strands stretching up and down the length of the old front porch.

Steve and I took in all this festivity with proverbial sugarplums dancing in our heads. Never had we known such a jolly time! We stayed out on the porch after the taffy had been laid, and began jumping back and forth over it, singing carols and feeling the magic in the air. "Look, it's snowing!" said Stephen, and the two of us looked at each other and shared a moment of pure, unadulterated joy. It is miraculous that we could have been so happy only months after we had lost our mom.

As we stood on the porch, the headlights of a station wagon lit the front yard as it pulled into the driveway. It was the Ryders, friends from down the road, coming to wish us all the greetings of the season. Steve and I ran into the house, heralding their arrival as though the three kings had shown up in the front yard.

Into the house they bustled, shaking off the snow at the door, and brought their packages into the living room. They had a bottle for Hal – which was quickly opened and used to toast the holiday – and their son Jeff gave me a little package. Red-faced, I opened it to find a small porcelain chickadee. It was beautiful, and everyone asked to see it. As it was passed around the room, I went back and forth between extremes of embarrassment and wonder. Jeff was much older than me, a handsome, rugged boy who had shown me, when we stopped in at their house once, how he had trained the birds in their backyard to come to his outstretched hand and take the seed he held.

We took our time saying goodbye to the Ryders as they bustled back out the front door that night, and Marnie asked me quietly if I had thanked Jeff for the gift. I had not, being much too embarrassed to say anything. "March yourself out there right now, young lady, and tell him thank you," she said, and I knew I had no choice. One did not wheedle when it came to Marnie. Mortified, I went out to the snowy driveway and said my tiny thanks. "Hey, you're welcome, kiddo," he grinned, and hopped into the car. My face was so red as to be burning, but I had done it. The car pulled away, with shouts of Merry Christmas mixing with the honking of the horn, and I returned inside to Marnie's hug. "You must always say thank you when someone does something nice," she whispered into my hair.

Christmas day was just this side of wacko. Where our Christmases in Connecticut had been fairly quiet, this was like a frenzy. Hal's mother was there – Nanny, she was called by everyone – and made a show of delivering her gifts to everyone. They were identical eggcups, and she delivered a whack to her daughter-in-law by saying that Marnie's gift had been broken. We laughed for years over that one. If they were all the same, how could she say with such certainty that it was Marn's that had cracked?

My most memorable gifts were the record album from my dad – Meet the Monkees – and the jackknife I got from Tommy. I was amazed that he knew how much I wanted one, and my feelings for him soared. Until years later when Harold, admitting he had told Tommy to buy the knife for me, ruined the whole entire thing.

I also got some homemade candy from my best friend Boo. It was some sort of caramel, colored blue and wrapped in individual bite-size pieces. I popped one in my mouth, savoring the buttery flavor – and promptly pulled my braces off my teeth with the first chew. I don't know if it was lucky or unlucky that Hal was a dentist. He brought me down the hall into his office, breathing bourbon-laced breath in my face, and began to correct the problem, all the while singing Christmas songs in his booming baritone.

By late morning, the living room looked like a bomb had gone off. Toddlers Annie and Tim were sitting in the middle of the bedlam, happily playing with their new toys. Carols rang through the air, accompanied by the crackle of the fire on the hearth. Later, a roast arrived at table, with Marn running the show. The jocularity was almost overwhelming, but I drank it in like a tonic, letting the emotion of my family wash over me.

Christmas 1967. Marnie at left. Harold in the back, Annie in front. Nanny is in the rocking chair

At the end of the day, when at last I was alone in my room over the office with my new treasures, I opened the pink diary I had gotten and wrote, "I still love you, Mom." I gazed at the words, my eyes clouding over with tears, and then I closed the little book, snapping the clasp shut, and put it and the matching pink pen in the drawer of my bedside table.

For many years after that, I would read those words in that book (I never wrote anything else in it, but not for any other reason than I could never keep up with diary or journal writing), and the flood of feeling from that night would come rushing back: the love and closeness of Christmas day, the safe and cozy feeling I had in Hal and Marnie's home, and the sense that everything was going to be ok.

Oblige me a brief digression, in which I will go on about someone who is not related to Marnie at all, who comes into her life toward the later end, and who seems neither to have influenced nor been influenced by her: Harold Chamberlin, Hal's son, who has influenced many of us in a fashion at once similar and entirely dissimilar to Marnie. It's just that, for me, the importance and weight of my year spent living on Old Sudbury Road cannot be parsed out into the fact of Harold and the fact of Marnie. It was a combination package.

Harold, Marn, and Harold's twin sister Cindy

Marn always called Harold "the Golden Boy." And he truly was, although maybe not in the way she meant it. Cute as all get-out, charming and friendly, he had a natural magnetism. For Marnie, though, he was someone to be kept on a short leash. Her calling him the Golden Boy reflected her frustration with him. He could seemingly do no wrong, especially in his father's eyes, and always got what he wanted, and this bugged her. She often suspected that he lied to her, and she was hard on him. He was given lots of chores, and she always held him to a very high standard. I suspect she was just not sure what to do with a boy, choosing to go with strictness. Still, he wormed his way into her heart, as he did with everyone.

When he was informed that we'd be moving in, I'm told Harold's first words were that Stephen could have his bedroom. He scarcely knew us, and he was already playing big brother. We three became, almost immediately, the best of friends. We were rarely apart, except when we were in school, as Harold was in Junior High, in a different building than Steve and I, in fourth and fifth grade respectively. And he sometimes had school things to go to after school or at night. He went to school dances — called Canteens — and drama club, playing Harry the Horse in the school production of Guys and Dolls that year. He was quite popular at school, and had more than a few girls interested in him. One time, a girl from the poorer side of town slipped me a note to give to him, basically offering herself to him in whatever way he wanted. It would have been so easy for Harold to take advantage of or ridicule this girl who, it was rumored, lived in a chicken coop. Instead, he sent me back with a message for her: "The feeling's mutual." Cheryl Godden, wherever you are now, you were a lucky girl to have picked Harold as your crush.

As charismatic as Harold was, though, he had a rather imbecilic side too; there was something endearingly innocent about him, a naiveté, as though he just didn't understand some very basic concepts. There is a story, for example, that Marnie came upon him one day, at about six years old, running round and round in tight circles in the yard. When she asked him what he was doing, he told her he was trying to run fast enough to see the back of his own head.

Harold had a keen sense of adventure, and often involved us in the kinds of hi-jinx that I would never have dreamed of doing otherwise. For a shy, quiet girl like me, things like sneaking into a drive-in movie, clambering over the chain-link fence at dusk and staying for the show, were not things I normally did. There was the time he talked Stephen and me into going sledding on a golf course near our house. We were having a fine time when the angry maintenance man came roaring out, yelling at us as he clomped over the snowy landscape. "Get out! Get out! You are ruining the course," He bellowed. I would have caved in horror, fear and embarrassment. Not Harold. "But sir," he said in his most earnest, endearingly imbecilic 12-year-old voice, "these sleds have the Miracle Plastic Edges." I couldn't believe it! What nerve he had! As I recall, however, this only made the maintenance man angrier.

We began to mentally catalog our adventures, giving them names and calling them "incidents." There was the fun but stupid incident, when we ventured onto the thin ice of a small pond, and the fun-but-scary incident, when someone saw us smashing a pumpkin on Halloween night and we had to race through the woods to avoid being caught.

I have no doubt that Harold was always aware that we were younger than he, and that we were his responsibility. I'm sure Marnie was not far from his thoughts in this regard! I always felt safe with him. It was such a good feeling to have someone older than me to depend on — I felt he would never put me in harm's way, and would take the lead in keeping us out of trouble, fearlessly taking stands against the likes of angry golf course maintenance men.

Lucky for me, the first boy I ever kissed was Harold, the summer after fifth grade, and we were to experiment a few baby steps further with intimacy the following summer. When Marnie caught us one morning – we had fallen asleep in the same bed – Harold's imbecile act worked on her, and there was no further mention of it. The fact that we were fully pajama-ed was a lucky break. Still, we knew we had dodged a bullet. Marnie's wrath was a force to be reckoned with, and this would have been a major transgression. One has to wonder if she knew something was up, but let it go. Perhaps she figured that Harold was a good choice for my intro to the world of boys. He was, after all, the Golden Boy.

It is probably a good thing that Harold's twin sister and older brother never lived with Marn. As tough as she was on Harold, she was even more so when it came to Cindi and Tom; she seems to have thought of Tom especially as pure trouble in the making. Whenever a police siren would be heard screaming up the road, Marn used to remark that Tommy must be in town.

Interestingly, both Tom and Cindi became champions of Marn in later years. To hear Cindi speak, you would have thought that Marn was right up there with the Mother Superior. She freely credits Marn with having taught her right from wrong — which reflects just as well on Cindi, for having risen to the occasion, as it does on Marn herself. During the year I lived with Marn in Wayland, Cindi would come visit on the weekends. I never really understood at the time what the deal was; the intricacies of divorce, custody and all that. All I knew was that every now and then I had my cousin to play with, a girl! For Cindi, it was a chance to be with our rollicking group, bombing around with Marn in her big yellow station wagon, and all of us singing. Marn used to claim she could come up with a song about anything, and she taught us kids dozens of them – Yellow Bird, Tom Dooley and Summer Time from Porgy and Bess. Often, in the middle of a conversation, she and Hal would look at each other and, in unison, say, "A song!," breaking then into whatever piece of music they had both just been reminded of.

Cindi also loved the chance to learn about cooking from Marn. Classic New England fare was a staple in that kitchen in Wayland: Casseroles, pot roasts, gravy as smooth as silk, and pies and cakes and steaming bowls of mashed potatoes. I remember her Boston baked beans and her London broil, always cut thin on the bias. I loved birthdays at her house, when she would make her special cake with the whipped chocolate frosting piled high. It seemed there was always something cooking in that little kitchen, and everyone had to go through the kitchen to get into the living room.

Marnie's bright, sunny living room. I can still picture it as though I was there yesterday. She had a special chair that was hers alone to sit in, and from that chair she dispensed her wisdom and her wit, usually with a cigarette and a bourbon within close reach. She bounced my baby sister Annie on her lap in that chair, playing Trot-Trot-to-Boston. She did her crossword puzzles, checked our homework and told Stephen and me stories about our mom. She would sometimes get very sad in the middle of a funny story, or find a reason to laugh in the middle of a sad one, and we always

Marn in her chair with Annie

soaked up those moments as though they were feeding our very souls.

It was a cozy room, but it could easily accommodate lots of people. It was a regular stop-off point for a couple of Hal's fly-fishing friends, who would happen by for a pop or two on the way home from work. From her throne, Marn presided over these often-boisterous gatherings – I think she may have invented Happy Hour. Issues were hotly debated, jokes were told, and the news of the day was tossed around, amid liberal doses of hearty laughter and swirls of tobacco smoke.

Sometimes, the men would stay long enough that their wives would call, looking for them; occasionally the wives even showed up, knowing that it was the place to be, and the hilarity would go late into the evening.

Marn never seemed to mind all the bedlam, and managed to keep an eye on us at the same time. She made sure we got our dinner and did our homework despite the wild party going on in the living room.

Another living room ritual was the passing of the train. The house was situated next to the train tracks, and the only train that ran on that line passed by every night at five o'clock. It was rare that the train went by without someone at the big living room windows, waving to the conductor. My baby sister Annie especially loved this little tradition.

On special occasions, Hal would light a fire on the big brick hearth, Marnie would turn the lights down low, and we'd have candles. It had such a magical ambience; it felt like being in church. And truly it was, for me, a place I think of today as having been holy.

Sometimes we kids would sing. We discovered early on that we were all musical; Harold played the clarinet in the school band, and was teaching himself to play his father's beautiful Martin guitar. Stephen and I had grown up singing with Mom, and so the three of us began copying Beatles songs. We practiced endlessly, learning harmonies and guitar solos up in Harold's little bedroom under the eaves. My dad had a reel-to-reel tape recorder at the time, and began recording us singing, dubbing in applause from one of Hal's Clancy Brothers records in between the numbers. He called us Harold and the Untouchables. We entertained the adults at many a cocktail hour in the living room, much to Marnie's delight. Being enamored of both music and us, she could not get enough of our singing, and encouraged us as though we were the next Simon & Garfunkel, all the while reminding us to enunciate the lyrics and not "swoop" up or down to notes.

So many things happened in that living room, including much of my healing after Mom's death. I think Marnie's heart was soothed by those warm, close times too. She regaled us with stories, saw to it that we remembered our manners, doled out love unconditionally and taught us so many lessons.

It wasn't all lessons and learning and powerful moments of course. There was a lot of just plain fun. There was the time Marn let me enter a contest to win a pony. Oh, how our hopes and prayers must have been at cross-purposes during the period while we waited to hear the winner announced! I didn't win, so Marn hit the jackpot – giving me a dream without having to deal with its coming true. Or maybe she just called the contest people and pulled my entry. But there was all kinds of Marnie-style fun. There were trips to the movies and special Sunday dinners. There were singalongs by the fireplace in winter and trips to Hal's old family farm in the summer.

Marn tried to give me some basic fashion pointers, but she was perhaps just a little too old to know what a girl my age might respond to, and I was a little too much of a tomboy to care anyway, but I do remember her talking about beauty. She would take me to see Frank, her hairdresser, and the two of them would confer on how best to feature my face. If anything, Frank was even more out of the loop than Marn on what the young girls were wearing, but I didn't really care. I loved how proud she was to introduce me to anyone who came into the shop. I would happily endure the attention of Frank just to get some of that wonderful feeling.

Just as she had been with her own three, Marnie was firm but fair with us. Looking back, I marvel – she suddenly had four children in her care, and that she was able to keep tabs on all of us is a wonder. At the time though, it really cut into my ability to live without consequences, and not being allowed to whine about it was most annoying.

I was invited, for example, to the birthday party of my friend Stephanie Burns. It meant a great deal to me, as I was new in town and had not made many friends. When the day came, and I was all ready with my wrapped gift and special outfit, Marn asked me casually if I had cleaned my room yet, as I had been told to. Hanging my head, I allowed as how I had not. Shaking her head, she said I was not going to the party. I had not done my chore, and I was to be punished for it. Imagine my disappointment! The mix of emotions was overwhelming, but, as was so often the case, I could not argue. She was, I knew even then, teaching me something important. You don't get to neglect your duties and still have your special treats. And so I trudged up the stairs to straighten my bedroom.

Unbeknownst to me, Marnie called Stephanie's mom, asking her to save a piece of cake for me, as I would be late.

When I was finished, some thirty minutes later, I came back down the stairs. Marn patted my head, told me I was a good girl, and that she would now take me to Stephanie's house. That birthday party was much more meaningful for me than it would have been without Marn.

Polly's eldest son Chip tells the story of sneaking out years later to call a "very hot" girl (Chip's words) on the pay phone at the library across the street from Marn's house. When he returned, he fell victim to Marn's sixth sense, and was forced to admit what he'd done. Her anger surprised him – while he was wrong to sneak around about it, she was not one to object to his having an interest in a girl. Turns out he had continued to chat after using up all his change in the phone, and in those days the phone company simply charged the other person's phone bill for any additional time. Marn was mad at him for making the girl's parents pay for his phone call. She disappeared up the stairs, coming down with a jar of change, and back across the street he went, armed for a lengthy chat. He has seen this girl since – she is now a born-again Christian, but, according to Chip, still smokin'.

Another time, Harold and Steve broke the glass part of the blender. They had taken it out of the dishwasher, still hot, and put milk and ice cream into it to make themselves a milkshake, causing the glass to crack. Thinking quickly (with a hearty dash of imbecile), they hid the broken piece under the daybed in the little playroom, never mentioning it to anyone. Except me. When, inevitably, Marn discovered it missing, she queried us about it, and Stephen owned up to the misdeed. The broken piece was retrieved from its hiding spot, still chocolaty from their attempt. Marn then turned to me, asking if I had known about it. Although most of the bones in my body were telling me to lie, I could not, and confessed that I had. I had not been a part of the crime, but I had been let in on it, so I was part of the cover-up.

Without missing a beat, Marn informed us that we would not be getting our allowance for the next two weeks, so that she could purchase a new blender. "Even me?" I asked. "Yes, Kimmie, you are as guilty as Harold and Steve, for keeping their secret." I glared at my brother and cousin, and we endured two whole weeks of no visits to Marshall's Apothecary to lay in candy supplies, and I had to wait another month before I had enough money saved up to buy the horse statue I had my eye on at the Ashley Shop.

The other thing I could not do was to argue with her. As infuriating as this was, however, I knew that her firmness was coming from a place of pure, fierce, tender love. It was a little confusing, to feel at once loved and punished. I felt oddly safe, and as much as I was stymied by her firmness, I was comforted by her fairness. She did not back down, but neither did she hold it against us. The discipline was kept in its place; it was swift and decisive, and then it was behind us, and we moved on, a little wiser, sometimes a little poorer, but always feeling loved.

In case we are treading too close to saintliness, I will point out that the woman had flaws, and being our stand-in mother – for us three young Harrises as well as Harold – was a big job. I do remember times when she was wrong, and I do not remember her ever owning up to those mistakes. One night, we were all goofing around – Stephen, Harold and I – right before bed. We had all had our showers and were in our pajamas. Marn was tidying up the bathroom after the calamity of the three of us taking our turns in there, and we were listening to a 45 on Harold's record player, leaping around the room and pretending to be Herman's Hermits. In the midst of the fun, and in the spirit of brotherly, fraternal shenanigans, Harold suddenly pulls Steve's pajama pants down. (I do not see how this kind of behavior is brotherly, or even a way to relate, but I am not a boy.) Mortified, Steve frantically grabs them back up, red-faced and sputtering, and turns on Harold. He is surprised to see Harold doing a modified version of the imbecile face, and so, utterly frustrated, he begins to cry. It is at this very moment that Marn joins the fray. She marches up to Stephen, which scares him a little in itself, and says in a stern voice, "Stephen, boys don't cry." His eyes shoot instantly over to me, as if to ask me, "Did she just say what I thought she said?" and "Is that right?" Marn, quickly turning into her Mary Poppins self, begins to spit-spot us into our beds, which for Steve and me means the meander through the house and out the long hallway of dental examination rooms, to the bedroom we shared over the office. Whether or not Marn realized her mistake upon seeing the shock on Steve's face, there was not another word on the subject.

And while we're here, I will add that she was sometimes harder on us than she needed to be. I've already said how she was with the three Chamberlin children, but Stephen and I were quiet, respectful, well-behaved kids, and still she cut us no slack. Here's an incident that illustrates this: There was a girl my age named Melany who lived up Old Sudbury Road from us, so Steve and I would sometimes go up to her house or she'd come down to ours. This girl Melany had a mouth like a sailor (to us kids anyway), using words – swears – that would never cross our lips in a million years. But even though we would not speak them, we still had a need to share the scandal of what we had heard, and so we wrote them on a piece of paper and showed Boo Bennett one day when she'd come by with her dad, who was one of the regulars at the happy hours in the living room. Although older, Boo was almost as innocent as we were, and so she was satisfyingly appalled at the thought of Melany's language. The three of us scoffed at anyone who would talk like that.

Later, as everybody was getting ready to leave, one of the other dads who had stopped by corralled us, saying Marn wanted to see us. We weren't exactly dragged in by our collars, but it had that kind of feel as we herded through the kitchen, into the dining room and toward her chair at the far end of the living room. There, in Marn's hand, was the piece of paper with Melany's swears on it. Instantly, I got a queasy feeling in the pit of my stomach and my knees felt a little weak. I gasped in air so I could squeak out an explanation; to explain our honor in writing, rather than speaking, the words on that page. But before I could get more than a few words out... Wham. There it was.

"I'm disappointed in all of you." There was more, but mostly I remember feeling terribly torn. Was this some kind of important lesson I needed to learn, or was she not giving me credit for being as good a kid as I was? I had learned by then that Marn possessed great wisdom, so how was I to process this experience? The three of us hung our heads low, but not before trying one more time to explain how virtuous we actually were. Our protests fell on seemingly deaf ears, and so we took our punishment. I don't remember what the punishment was, but I do remember thinking it was pretty light for old Marn, so maybe that was her mute acquiescence.

When our year with Marn was over, Steve and Annie and I returned to our home in Connecticut. It was at this point that life got tougher for me. The reality of my mother's death became more than something to talk about; I was really alone.

Those were hard times for me, but once again, Marn stayed in close touch and kept me anchored. My father hired a succession of housekeepers to watch us while he was at work, and I began to try and make my way back into a world far from Wayland and Marnie's house.

Stephen and I and spent several weeks with her that next summer vacation, and spent the year between writing letters back and forth with Harold, making plans to buy some electric guitars, amps and microphones when we had saved up enough money. The letters back and forth, and the memories of all our adventures from the year before, sustained me until I could be at Marn's again.

That summer was so much fun! We did get those instruments and ramped up Harold and the Untouchables – the volume of it anyway. But much of the enjoyment came from just being around Marn. She had such a reassuring way, and such a sunny outlook on life. I loved spending as much time with her as I could.

She was driving to the farm stand one morning, and asked if I would come along. Of course I said yes, knowing that, whenever you set foot out the door with Marn, there was a chance you might be in for some fun.

As we turned on to the old farm road, Marn and I passed a very athletic woman jogging briskly along the road. "Oh, Kimmie," sighed Marn, "Wouldn't you love to be able to run like that?" I did not respond beyond a "Hmm" because, being 13, I was perfectly capable of running like that.

Walking into the stand, all the ladies behind the cash register waved good morning to Marn, and they tossed little comments back and forth with her about the weather. She inquired as to what was fresh, and they steered her to the first aisle. There a lady greeted her by name. "Well, hi, Midge!" she exclaimed. Marn said hi back, and they wished each other a happy Fourth of July. As we walked away, she whispered to me, with a look of mock horror on her face, that she had no idea who that was.

She picked out corn, cucumbers and scallions, finding a second pile of scallions farther down that seemed better than the first pile, so she sent me back with the first batch. There was a young man eyeing the first batch of scallions as I dropped ours on the pile, and Marnie called over to me, telling me to alert him to the better pile. I just looked at him, and he turned his attention to her, somewhat unsure but willing to follow her, much as we all were.

As we paid for our purchases, the woman behind the counter put the fruits and vegetables into brown paper bags, and handed one to me, saying, "Comme ça." I recognized the expression right away from our time in Switzerland, where I had learned to speak French quite well. Seeing my surprised look of comprehension, she continued, "Parlez-vous Français?" I'm sure I blushed, never wanting to be focused on in a crowd, but managed to say, "Un petit peu," hoping she would not continue. She beckoned to me with a crooked gardener's finger to come around the side of the counter. When I did, she showed me a litter of tiny newborn kittens in a big straw basket. Marn came around too, and let out a sound that was part harrumph, part guffaw. "Don't be getting any ideas, lovey," she said. "We do not need any cats in our house."

A cat strolled into our midst as Marn returned to her packages. It twined around my legs and then stretched itself up my bare leg and let out a yawn. The woman tapped me on the shoulder and said (I think), "Elle vous aime!" Marnie called to me just then to get the door on the car, and I smiled at the woman, giving her a little wave as I ran off gratefully to help. I thought to call out an au revoir, but I didn't want to keep the exchange going, and besides, I thought it might come out sounding dumb.

Marn and I piled everything into the car and were off. As we drove away, the same jogger was still running along, now coming toward us, so that we could see her face. "How sad," said Marn, "All that exercise hasn't done much for her looks."

A little farther along, we saw taillights coming on as people ahead of us slowed their cars. There was some commotion causing everyone to creep by. When we got close enough to get a look, we could see a newborn foal with its mother not far from the fence at the roadside. "Oh, Kimmie! Let's have a look."

She pulled the car over onto the soft shoulder of the road, and I jumped out and dashed for the fence, Marnie close behind. We stood, watching the baby horse spindle around on its impossibly skinny legs, while its mother nuzzled it gently. A woman came walking up from behind the stables, wearing mucking boots and gloves. As she came closer, she pulled the gloves off and called to us. "Hiya, Midge," she said, and pointed at me. "Would she like to come in and give our new baby a pat?" Mouth open, I looked up at Marn, who inquired to be sure that both mother horse and baby horse would be gentle, and then nodded. "How very kind of you, Janet," she said, helping me open the double gate along the driveway. She called out an introduction as I walked slowly toward the horses, and the woman and I shook hands. She was a patient of Hal's, and asked me if I was familiar with horses. I told her that I had taken riding lessons in Connecticut. As I approached, she held out a bit of apple. "Give this to Martha," she said, pointing to the mare, "So she'll know you're a friend." Martha seemed quite uninterested in both me and the apple, but the foal was very inquisitive. She wobbled over to us, sticking her neck out to reach me with her grey nose. I opened my hand and she tickled it with her lips. She had a blaze of bright white down her caramel face, and huge dreamy eyes. "We're thinking of calling her Sunny," said the woman, laying a comforting hand on the mare's broad back. I reached out and touched Sunny's neck, patting her softly. She tossed her exquisite head and pricked her ears at me. "I think she likes you, Kimmie!" cheered Marn from the fence.

The woman left me as she wandered the few feet away to chat with Marn. Meanwhile, Sunny and I bonded for life in an ecstatic few moments, as I patted her head, stroked her neck, and even scratched around her ears a little. Martha stood by, every bit the maternal figure, but content to let me stay. The clouds overhead coursed across the summer sky. Butterflies flitted around in the mild breeze, landing on the vibrant Indian Paintbrushes growing in the field. I was in love.

It was a short-lived romance, for within a few minutes Sunny bounded away, running and kicking awkwardly in crazy circles. The women laughed and I trotted back to the fence. We jumped into the car, after I bashfully thanked Janet and shook her hand. Just then, the clouds began to darken and big fat raindrops began to fall on our windshield.

"Well! Wasn't that fun?" said Marn, smiling at me as she put the wipers on. By the time we drove out to the main road, the rain was picking up, and was soon coming down in sheets. I could not have cared less, except to be glad it had waited until after I met Sunny and Martha.

As we rounded the corner onto Old Sudbury Road, Marn drove straight through the biggest curbside puddle, a treat we had enjoyed with her since we were very small. The water splashed up alongside the car window, and Marnie said, "Whee!"

It may not have been skydiving, but you never knew what might happen when you went out with Marnie.

We got home, and after bringing in the bags from the farm stand, I ran up to my room and flopped on my bed. I pulled out a pad and a pencil and began to do a sketch of Sunny. I drew about ten pictures of Sunny. I tried to draw myself into the pictures, but I wasn't that good on people, so I kept erasing myself. Soon Harold and Stephen came barreling up the stairs. They flopped on the beds too, asking where we'd been. I told them about Sunny, and Steve was very impressed. Harold not so much, but he could see that it meant a lot to me, so he said, "Neat."

We all eventually trundled back down the stairs in search of lunch. Marn had put all the vegetables away, and was starting to get out sandwich stuff. We ate a lot of peanut butter and jelly that summer, and watermelon, peaches and popsicles. The three of us sat down at the little white kitchen table and chowed down, Harold and Steve snickering into their milk glasses about some idiotic thing that had happened while Marn and I were gone. "Would you boys care to share what is so funny?" she asked. They looked at each other, still stifling giggles, but realizing they had better tone it down, because the thing they were laughing at was not appropriate for Marnie's ears. "It was really nothing," they said almost in unison, which gave us something we could all laugh about. "You sound as if you've been rehearsing that all morning," she said, batting one of them in the back of the head with a hot pad. "Now eat up, all of you. I have a little chore for this afternoon." Suddenly the giggling stopped, and our eyes all met. Nothing good could come of this, we thought. Rather than eating up, we slowed down, but we were really finished eating, and we looked up at Marnie.

Never one to beat around the bush, she said, "I want the cellar cleaned out." I am surprised; I never even knew there was a cellar, and I can only imagine what this job is going to entail.

Hal came in at this point, taking his lunch break from the office. He grabbed Marn from behind, wrapping his arms around her and singing a silly song. "Oh, Hal, stop it," said Marn. "My back." He backed away then, doing a little teasing imitation of her behind her back. She told him that we were going to clean out the cellar, and he sang another song, something about a poor little chore girl.

Marn marched us out the back door, into the still-cloudy-but-not-raining-any-more day, and around to the back of the house. There were the bulkhead doors that I might have noticed if I ever went back there. Harold pulled them open, revealing a dank staircase going into blackness. A workman's light — the kind with a light bulb inside a wire cage and a big hook on the top — was found and lit, and we could see that it was actually a fairly small space. We began pulling junk out and depositing it in the yard, and it started to get kind of fun. Marn was supervising, and we got the giggles as we tried on old army helmets and rode around on rusty tricycles. By late afternoon we had gotten everything back in its place, and lots of stuff for the trash man to haul away.

"Now," said Marn, "how would this be for a little club house for you three?" We looked at each other with the same thought: Cool! The late day sun finally made an appearance, streaming through the trees as we bolted back down the steps and began pulling stumps and wooden crates out for tables and chairs. "Just be sure and wash up when you come in," said Marn as she climbed the steps to go inside.

For dinner that night, we had the corn and cucumbers from the farm stand, along with Marn's famous London broil, sliced thin on the bias. And by the end of the summer, we had set up an authentic garage band scene in the cellar, with our electric guitars, amps and microphones, and even a makeshift drum set, and were having the time of our lives. We performed as an electrified group for the first time at Marnie's surprise 60th birthday, over at Susan and Tom's house in Sudbury. The mikes shorted out once or twice, and Marnie hated that she couldn't hear the words, but we rocked.

The following summer, Marn and Hal took my brother and sister, Harold and Cindy, our cousin Tim, who is about Annie's age, and me, on a camping trip in the Audubon Wildlife Sanctuary in Wellfleet on Cape Cod. So, if you didn't count it up yourself, I'll do it for you: there were six children between the ages of about 13 and 4 to care for, the littlest ones still having to take naps. Our campsite looked like a settlement, with tents large and small, clotheslines, food being served around the clock, and of course the camper. But boy, did we have a blast! We spent our days exploring the tide pools, woods and beaches, falling into our sleeping bags each night exhausted. Us older kids were given a measure of freedom, being allowed one day to rent bicycles and ride on the bike path to Provincetown, all by ourselves. It was quite a distance – maybe 7 or 8 miles – and just breathtakingly beautiful. The trail was laid out so that there were spots where you rode downhill into a shady stand of trees, and you'd get a little chill after being in the sun. But the perfect little paved path just wound around the trees and back up, popping you into the dazzling sunlight again and up to where it was just sand dunes as far as you could see. We sang as we rode along, imagining that we were a famous singing group making a movie. Our song for a capella times like that was almost always "Love Is Blue," with no lyrics, just "ba – ba – ba" in three parts.

Once we made it to town, we stocked up on penny candy at the shop in the center of P-town (which is still there today), and later met up with Marnie and Hal, who drove to town with the little ones and bought us all hamburgers at a roadside stand. I'll never forget the feeling of freedom we had that day, as though we might travel on our bikes all the way to Paris if we wanted. As it was, Provincetown in the late 1960s was plenty exotic for us — with all the crazy beatniks and their bongo drums, it was a pretty wild place — and I marvel that Marn let us taste that freedom.

Once my family was out of Marnie's hair – and her house – she began to relax and enjoy life. Harold was still there of course, but he was the oldest of all of us, and there was only one of him. She fixed up the house a bit; making our playroom into her "office," with a little wicker desk painted white, white, white with lime green accents. It was from here that she wrote her letters to us.

This was a wonderful time in Marn's life. She and Hal were having a ball, and she could keep up with him despite the ten years she had on him. Her worries were behind her now. No more lying awake at night, wondering how she was going to manage. No more hiding from the bill collector.

And she embraced it! She sized up her circumstances, and decided to enjoy the hell out of life. Because, as you know by now, Marnie was game. And she had the freedom, at this point in her life, to let herself live a little. She never forgot where she came from — and she never forgot Linda — for a minute. But our Marn was going to reach for the brass ring, and she came into her own during this time, putting the finishing touches on her extraordinary life story.

She was in her element in a boisterous, convivial crowd, and was especially good at starring in the show. She loved laughs, grins and hilarity in any form. How many times did she hold court in my presence! And many more that

I've heard tell of. Her style was not loud – she didn't catch people's attention by shrieking or making a scene, but capture them she did, making for more memorable evenings than anyone can remember.

Marn, Linda's son Stephen and Hal

She would have had to like wild times to marry Hal, a guy who was on a constant quest for fun. In many ways, it was a great match. Together, they went on jaunts, trips and cruises, always having a high old time. They especially loved meeting people, and they met them everywhere they went. They would sit at the bar in a pub, in Ireland, Bermuda or Boston, chatting with the bartender, and by the end of the evening, they would have dozens of new friends.

Then there were all the times she and Hal would sit at piano bars, leading the crowd in song. They both had the same absolute love for music as well as the ability to belt out a good tune. They also had an impressive repertoire, so they could keep the piano player company for hours. A song would be suggested by someone and launched into, and Marn would be transformed. She would get a very light expression on her face – eyebrows raised, with a little smile, and her head tilted to the side just a bit – as she warbled along in her pitch-perfect little cigarette-influenced alto and Boston brogue.

The piano players always enjoyed this company because they would get the crowd going, enticing other patrons to sidle up to the piano until there was a raucous crowd. Free rounds would be called for, along with much raising and clinking of glasses, all of which must have resulted in good tips for the piano man.

Of all the places they traveled to, Bermuda was Marnie's all-time favorite place to go. Imagine! Our Marn, in Bermuda! I'm sure, back on Moore Road, or living with Aunt Mary and Aunt Rose, that she never dreamed she'd end up a lady who vacationed in Bermuda! She and Hal went there a lot, often bringing along miscellaneous children and grandchildren. They would stay at their favorite hotels and guesthouses, dine in their favorite restaurants and, of course, visit every bar there was to visit. By the end of each stay, they would have a whole cadre of new friends. But they were also always a hit with waiters, bartenders and hotel staff. Marnie really took an interest in the help, asking people who waited on her about their families and such, a habit that endeared her to many a waitress and chambermaid.

On one such trip, she and Hal got it into their heads to throw a party for the staff at the hotel. They had particularly enjoyed their stay that year, and wanted to do something special. And just a little bit zany. Lord knows how they arranged this, but they got a bunch of booze and good food delivered to the bungalow they were staying in, and had a wild night dancing and singing and drinking with the staff, to thank them for their hospitality.

Polly and Susan's families figured into Marnie's life much more prominently than Linda's did after she died. My father was very good to bring us to family events at Marn's, even after he had remarried, but it was not the same. There was no longer the connection of Linda to tie us in, so our times with our family became fewer and farther between. I don't remember any Christmases, and very few Thanksgivings with Marn after the year we lived there, and we were never a part of those trips to hither and yon. How I would love to be able to tell you about them, because it would mean I was there. I know they would have done a world of good for me, as I was rather adrift in the world for many years.

And yet Marn did her best to keep us on her radar screen. She often asked for Annie over school vacations after Steve and I had gone off to college. So Annie got to have some special times with her cousins, and I know it was special for both Annie and Marnie. Especially Marnie. As a toddler, Annie's adorable little face had helped Marn through those first days after Mom's death; she had a very special place in her heart for my sister. But she was starting to get older, making her a little less in tune with the youngsters.

Marnie's grandchildren, 1975

Old Marn wasn't quite ready to be put out to pasture just yet though! She could still be a force in the lives of her grandchildren, teaching the next generation in the same unique manner that she had employed with her own children. One time Susan's older child, Tim, was hanging out with my sister at Marn's house – they were around 13 or 14 (not much older than I'd been when I got caught for writing Melany's bad language on the slip of paper). Marn could hear, with her supersonic ears, that Tim was talking about sex. She called the two of them into the living room and instructed Tim to get the dictionary. Once he returned with it, she asked him to please look up the word intercourse and read the definition aloud. Then he was to look up masturbation and read that one out loud too. I don't know how many words she gave him, but his face probably stayed red for days after.

As she got older, I believe that Marnie did begin to fade from the lives of her younger grandchildren, but the older ones had the benefit of the bonds built in years past when she herself was younger and had more vitality. We were perhaps easier to relate to as we became young adults. I know that I was always absolutely sure of her – that her love for me transcended everything, and that she was always just a phone call away. Maybe that was more important to me than to my other cousins, who still had mothers, or, in the case of my younger siblings, who still had me. But for a young teenaged girl maneuvering out into the world on feet that had had the rug pulled out from under them, with no role model (save Harold), and little emotional support to speak of at home, knowing Marnie was there for me meant the world. My father's second marriage was a rocky, unhealthy one, making my lack of a sense of security or safety even more raw and frightening, but I never picked up the phone and called her during those awful years. Just knowing she was there, like a parachute whose ripcord I could pull at any time if things got too dangerous, a safety net whose presence I always knew was there, was enough to comfort me.

Meanwhile, the adventure that was Marn's life was continuing. In the late 70's, Polly, Susan and Marn began going on what they called "Spring Flings." They would run off for a long weekend, usually to Cape Cod, hole up in a motel and play bridge. (They would bring along a friend to make a foursome.) It was a chance for the little family to be together again, without husbands and children, and reconnect. There was always a lot of booze flying around at these gatherings, and the stories of their exploits – venturing out for dinner or shopping – included much hilarity. They went to a bar in Falmouth once, and were already several sheets to the wind by the time the piano player began his first set. They listened politely to the first few numbers, but eventually they were singing along, swaying from side to side on their bar stools, and calling out requests. The gent took a break and sat at the end of the bar, as far away from them as possible. They arranged to send him a cocktail, and asked him after a time if he was going to play more. "Are you," he responded in a clipped voice, "going to sing?"

There were several times as a teenager that I found myself out in a bar with Marnie and Hal, and the two of them absolutely enchanting the other patrons, and me of course. People were constantly amazed that this was my grandmother. One time, I remember spying Marn across the crowded room at a big keg party at the cottage Harold was renting for the summer, up in Ogunquit, Maine. I was about 17 at the time of this party, and across the room I saw that Marn was deep in conversation with Rick, my boyfriend at the time. As I looked more closely, I could see she was crying. Shit, I thought, and I zoomed over. Rick looked up at me, a little misty-eyed himself, and said, "I love your grandmother." Turns out, she had been telling him about my mom, and got carried away. But she was a great storyteller, even with a few pops in her, and I'll bet Rick has never forgotten that moment, so moved was he by the story she told.

In our later teens, Harold and Stephen and I took to playing our music in the occasional bar or coffee house, singing many of the same songs we had learned on Old Sudbury Road. And from time to time, Marn was in the audience. She would listen to us with a mildly nervous expression on her face, as though she was willing us not to make a mistake or sing a flat note. There was a talent show we entered, at the legendary Fan Club in Ogunquit, that same summer of the keg party. Harold and I had summer jobs in town, and Marn and Hal brought Steve up for the weekend so he could sing with us.

The night of the talent show, Marn made a big fuss over our outfits. We were a little too old for her to be dressing us, but it was kind of fun. Harold and Steve wore bow ties and I wore a big flowered muumuu that was my mother's. We practiced a little bit outside in the weeds behind the bar, and then went on stage. We were competing against Broadway actors and talented drag queens, but somehow we won, singing "California Dreamin'." Well, Marnie just about busted a gut. She was beaming all over the place, telling the other patrons that we were her grandchildren. She even managed to be quoted in the Boston Herald the next day, telling the reporter that we hadn't been at our best that night. That kind of fan adoration you just can't buy.

Sometime in 1976, I brought a boyfriend named Schmidty to meet Marn. He was a nifty guy, and I thought they'd hit it off. Although it was only early afternoon, Marn offered him a drink, and he accepted a hefty tumbler of scotch. We all chatted and giggled together; Marn bragged at one point that she could think of a song on any topic you could come up with, and I suggested farts, for which I got a disdainful "Kimmie!" Some weeks later, I received a note from Marn, saying that, while she found him to be a very nice young man, he was not the right one for me.

As it turned out, the one I picked was also not the right one for me, but he had everyone snowed for a while with his charm and social nature. Marn referred to him as a "Junior Palmer," a little joke on Palmer, Jr., and high praise at that point, as she had come around to being very fond of her youngest son-in-law.

I remember a time when I would have said that Marn dropped completely out of my life for a while, but the truth is, it is the other way around; I dropped out of hers. I was going to college in Boston, wrapped up in my own little world, too busy to be thinking of my grandmother. One day, the phone rang in the messy-but-organic kitchen of the hippy collective household where I was living. I answered it, and who should it be but Marnie. She was calling because it had been ten years to the day since my mother's death. So caught off guard was I by her call that I made some glib remark in response, essentially telling her that family was no big deal to me. The call was very brief, but a few days later another one of those cards arrived for me in the mail. It was from Marnie, and it read, "You may think that I have so many loved ones around me, so much love in my life, I probably have enough. But I need your love too, Kimmie." Well, that hit me like a ton of bricks, but a very soft and loving ton of bricks. She was letting me know that I had done wrong, but the wrong itself was as simple as not giving her my love.

There was a very festive family occasion around that time that I was a part of, being Polly and Palmer's 20th Anniversary. Marn and Hal were there, and it was a party in the classic family tradition, complete with singing, screaming laughter, drinking and lots and lots of love.

When I told Marn that I was to be married, she was just so thrilled. I think she thought I had chosen someone who would take care of me and with whom I would have a fun life.

It was she who took me shopping for my wedding dress – after I showed her the one I had picked out which was completely inappropriate. We got into Hal's red BMW Bavaria one fine day – mind you, this was a showpiece car whose engine he routinely hand-polished – and headed out toward Rt. 128 and Jordan Marsh. As we hit the modest limited-access highway, Marn began to accelerate – telling me it was good for the car to hit 100 miles per hour from time to time. I laughed somewhat nervously as the speedometer crept up, and I was ever so relieved when it began to come back down.

Marn knew I was going for the "sunset on the beach" kind of wedding rather than anything traditional. Still, she made me try on a few horrifying items that day. I would come out of the dressing room all covered in a whipped cream vision of a dress, and she would gasp and clasp her hands at her throat, saying, "Oh, Kimmie! Look how pretty!" My retort would let her know in no uncertain terms that there was no way I was going to be seen in this get-up, and she'd sigh, shooing me off to try on the next one. It was really just a game, and I played along, allowing myself to be humiliated by trying on dreadful dresses so she could pretend her granddaughter was the kind of girl who would want to wear clothes like that. We ended up buying one that was almost as wrong as the original, but a little more formal, and something we both liked.

I was so happy to have her spend the night before my wedding at my father's house, with all of us laughing and singing late into the night. The next morning, I took a walk down the old road my folks lived on, thinking about this big step I was taking. As I came up the road on my return, I heard her little voice come chirping from the guest room window, calling, "Good morning, Bridie!" It was not a good marriage, but I'm glad Marn was there for the wedding.

In 1984, Marnie went into the hospital for gall bladder surgery. It was to signal a marked downturn in her health. For one, she had a bad reaction to the anesthesia – some said she never recovered from it. She became weak and sometimes confused. She pulled some crazy stunts during that time, which became very funny stories after everything came out okay each time. One time, she took the car and drove out the driveway before Hal could stop her. She drove herself to the bank and pulled up to the drive-through window, where she waited to be attended to. After a while, the throngs of people standing inside the bank looking at her told her something was amiss, and she realized she had pulled up not to the drive-through, but just to some arbitrary window, driving up across the grass to do so. She continued on to the gas station, from where Hal, now mildly frantic, received a phone call. It was George Sheppard, an old boyfriend of Linda's, calling to say Mrs. Chamberlin was there acting strangely. When Hal arrived at the garage, Marn was sitting in the driver's seat of her car, looking very surprised to see him. She swore she had done nothing out of the ordinary and drove off in a huff. Thankfully, she headed home.

I remember a visit to her house on Old Sudbury Road when my daughter was a baby. I was in her little kitchen, fixing us some sandwiches, when Marn walked into the room, carrying a very small mitten. "We don't know whose mitten it is," she said absently. She stood there for a moment, looking at the little mitten in her fingers, and then turned and went back to her chair in the living room. It was sad – and maybe a tiny bit funny, but mostly sad — to see her this way.

That was the year the Robinson girls went to Mystic, Connecticut for what was to be their last Spring Fling. Marn was very sick, but she really wanted to go, and so go they did, bringing Polly's friend Arlene along as the fourth for Bridge. Once they arrived in town, they tried to find something that Marn could drink. She had lost her taste for her beloved bourbon, so an alternative needed to be found. They settled on some sort of flavored champagne, and brought it back to the motel. The four played bridge into the evening and got snockered – the usual routine – having a general blast. When Marn said she was ready to go to bed, Polly and Susan tried to discourage her, telling her to have another drink, have a smoke, and play another round. Finally, Arlene, who had been watching the whole scene, said, "Aren't we supposed to be keeping her alive?"

What was more significant than the ravages of her illness, however, was the fact that Hal had become interested in another woman. His new receptionist, a buxom woman named Mary, became his new distraction, and he had begun spending time with her while Marn was in the hospital for the gall bladder issue. Initially, it appears that she knew nothing about this, just noticing changes in the way he dressed and in his interest in, for instance, getting a suntan. She told people he was becoming foolish and laughed about it a lot. But it is clear that, by the time she died, she knew he was cheating on her.

It is fair to ask why this should have surprised her. After all, she had done the same thing. Trust me when I say it was different. She was deeply hurt. We all were. Many say Marn died of a broken heart… but I don't think the congestive heart failure helped.

She was rushed back to the hospital some six months after the gall bladder surgery, this time for heart and lung problems. She was in intensive care for a month, and the family took turns visiting with her there. Her demeanor improved while there; everyone noticed that she was nicer. She even seemed to let Hal off the hook, although her memory was fading, and so she may simply have forgotten that she was mad at him.

When at last she was well enough to come home, relatives came from far and wide to welcome her. Her grandchildren made a big welcome home sign and stuck it up on the front porch. When Hal got her out of the car, however, all Marnie could see were the porch stairs, which she was never going to be able to scale. She burst into tears and slumped against Hal. Polly told her not to worry; grandson David would carry her up the stairs. But no, she wanted to do it herself, and somehow she found the strength to climb them, holding Polly's hand for moral support. They helped her into the living room and onto the couch, where she immediately fell asleep. The bi-fold doors between the living room and kitchen were closed, and a blasteroo of a party proceeded to take place. Big pots of food were prepared, laughter flowed, and music and merriment were made into the night, through which Marn slept.

That was just before Christmas. Everyone knew full well it was to be her last one, and so they pulled out all the stops. Hal nailed a long board on the mantelpiece to accommodate the many stockings, and Marn languished on the couch while all around her the chestnuts were roasted, carols sung and packages exchanged. It was on Christmas night that Marnie told Kathy McGloin, an old family friend, that she was not afraid to die. She was just, she said, not quite ready for it. There was still so much more to see, especially where her grandchildren were concerned.

She made it another couple of months, and then went back into the hospital. These were to be her final weeks on earth, and she went in and out of consciousness as family rushed to be by her side. The weekend before she died, Polly came up from New York and Chip came down from school, and the two of them spent hours making shamrock cards from construction paper for all of Marn's nurses. (This was Marn's idea, not Polly's, and certainly not Chip's. They couldn't believe how they were roped into this inane task by the dying matriarch.) Polly's youngest, Jeffrey, also came for a visit, and told Marn that he had been accepted into Hartwick College. "Oh, the finest college in the world!" was her response, and she told all the nurses who came by that day that her grandson was going to Harvard. No one corrected her.

After Polly had been there a few days, Palmer called and told her to come home. Her family needed her, he said. Polly was so distressed to leave her mother, knowing she might never see her again, but she acquiesced to her husband, in turn telling Chip, who was missing college so he could stay by Marn's side, that he needed to leave too. There was simply not much anyone could do as she languished, and the pluck for which she was known was there less and less.

Pluck is strong stuff though, and it never disappeared completely. Before he left, Chip went to her bedside one more time. She was unresponsive, with her eyes closed. "Say something to her, Chip," said Polly, seated nearby. "Maybe she'll hear you." Chip thought about this for a moment. "Marnie," he began, "if you open your eyes, I'll give you a bourbon." If you think she did not open her eyes then and there, you have not been paying attention.

Polly and Chip went their separate ways, and Marn passed away a few days later. Susan was there, and Hal. And also, apparently, Hal's new friend Mary.

I was not around for the end of Marnie's life. It pains me to say this. I was dealing with my own stuff, and I missed many special times. For this, I am sad. But even though I knew she was in the hospital, I never believed she would die. For one, she had been in hospitals so many times over the years. But there was also her invincibility. She made it through so many things, and always with a confident air and a smile. Her strength was the stuff of legends. How could something like death beat her?

Of course it did.

What do you suppose the family did at this point? Not at all what you might guess, but maybe you can understand this unorthodox chronology, now that you know the family: they all went to Bermuda. The trip had been a Christmas present for all the Sealy and Shepard kids, who had been beside themselves with excitement ever since. And in what may have been Marnie's last wispy little words, she whispered to Polly on the phone the day before her death, "Just think! In two days, you'll be up in the air on your way to Bermuda." And so they went, leaving Susan home to make the final arrangements. And it was by all accounts a wonderful trip – lots of laughter, a few tears, and general wild times – and Polly talked to Susan on the phone every day.

I already told you, way back at the beginning, about Marn's memorial service. It was, in the tradition of the family, a Quaker service, held at the Martha Mary Chapel, where all the weddings had taken place. The chapel was full to brimming, and people got up and said lovely things about our Marn…. Or so I'm told – as I mentioned, I don't remember anything about it, so desperately sad was I. She had died young, at 73, and left a huge hole in the hearts of so many, especially me.

We went on to have our 'Family Frolics' at Polly and Palmer's home on Long Island, as well as other get-togethers, and they were always a great time. It seemed a natural part of those times to keep Marn's memory alive, through telling the stories of her life and the lessons we learned from her. We each had our own special connection to her – she left us with so much to remember her by!

She had sayings, phrases that she repeated to us all, which were meant, I think, to teach us small lessons in life. She used lots of expressions that are not heard today, but which were popular in her day. "Lord love a duck," a fairly common expression in Cockney circles in England, and used by James Joyce in Ulysses, was a Marnie-ism. So was "pish tosh." And she used expressions like "It's not from the wind she gets it," "The sun is over the yardarm," and "There but for the grace of God go I," but there were other, more obscure

references too. For example, if someone asked her for one too many favors, she would put on her most ladylike face and calmly say, "How are you fixed for spit?" A person who was overcome by lightheadedness (or alcohol, embarrassment or passion) was said to have "a touch of the vapors." A drink, of any size, might be called "a wee drop of the creature," said in an Irish brogue. Then there was "May as well be hung for a sheep as a lamb," which I took to mean that there's no point in going half-way; if you are going to do something, go for broke.

One of her most interesting Marnie-isms was The Tender Trap. Any guesses as to what the tender trap is? Not what you might think, especially coming from our Marnie: It is motherhood. That is the tender trap. A trap, according to the dictionary, is a strategy or mechanism designed to ensnare. Using trickery, artifice or allure, it snaps shut, catching its prey unawares. The tender trap, Marnie said, is set even before pregnancy, as a happy young couple dream of their future family. Once the child is born, the jaws of the trap are closing around its mother's ankles, while she blissfully makes eyes at her progeny and its father. By the time the house is filled with screaming children in need of diaper changing, rides to the library and cleaning, it is too late, and she lives in the trap for the rest of her life.

We discussed this at dinner last night. How funny, we thought, that someone who lived so entirely for family used such a phrase, and used it often enough that we all remember it. We decided that it was one of her rare moments of commenting on the big picture, that she saw child-rearing — especially the woman's part in it — for the trap it was, keeping people tied to each other, keeping women tied to the home and the children. Indeed, we speculated, it is what constitutes a family, making the trap responsible for that fundamental unit that holds our entire culture together. This is pretty deep for old Marn.

I like the idea of these sayings, these quotations. When looked at as a whole, they say a lot about the person who was known to say them. The familiarity of them became something like a nursery rhyme – a sing-songy, repetitive metaphor or warning. When she told Harold not to eat the flowers, he knew she was growing tired of him scraping his spoon across his empty cereal bowl, trying to get the last bits of milk, as though he were trying to eat the flowers painted on the dish itself. I'm sure he hears her saying it to this day. Perhaps he has even found himself saying it, or at least thinking it, when he experienced someone else, like one of his kids, going for that last bit of gravy on a dinner plate. When Marnie said, "Don't teach your grandma how to suck eggs," we knew that we were coming close to that worst of offenses – disrespect – by trying tell a grown-up how to do something. The expression "The hell with it if you have to go to the cellar for it" was the punch line of a long-forgotten joke, but was used in numerous ways.

Marnie taught love well. She just really understood it. It was from her that I learned that you can love someone even when you don't like him or her very much. This ties in with her authenticity – she was never phony, but she never stopped loving me, even when I wasn't very likeable. She just let me know that I was being horrid, and the love part was understood.

She taught about family through everything she ever did. As a young mother, she admonished her children (and I admonished mine) to save their best behavior of all for when they were at home, and she assured her daughters on a regular basis that family was always safe. They could tell her anything, no matter what it was. Family was her religion.

And she taught about happiness and spirit and fun. Oh, how she taught about happiness and spirit and fun. On this subject, she said simply, "If you're not happy, do something about it." She was not attached to material possessions save the few things she was planning to leave each of us when she died. (For me, it was a little writing desk, which has had a label in it identifying it as mine since I was ten years old. Today, it is in my dining room) But the invisible threads connecting us to each other meant the world to her.

Her spirit saw her through so many tough times, and became like an aura around her as she grew old....

Her daughters all inherited Marn's love of fun too, and instilled it in their kids in turn. Family gatherings were, and continue to be, hilarious and wildly fun. All of us have friends who say they would kill to have a family like ours, and I know what they mean. On the night of Susan's memorial service, we were kicked out of a bar en famille for excessive jocularity, and we've been chastised by clergy for disrupting ceremonies, but our kind of fun seems rarely to be irritating to those around us – except the owners of the restaurants or the minister trying to get through a wedding rehearsal. On the contrary, people often join in the fun, singing along or clapping at our various and occasional performances. It is infectious, this fun that Marnie's family spreads in the world.

Marn felt that the addition of fun to one's life is a choice, but if you make the commitment to finding fun, you will enhance your experience mightily. The next time you are in a restaurant, try ordering your meal in a funny voice; at least a British accent if you are not bold enough to do an impression of Dudley Do-Right or Vladimir Putin. Ask waitpeople about their families, something Marn often did. If you can do harmony, try singing together as you walk down the street. I will stop short of suggesting you disrupt religious ceremonies, but there are endless ways to create fun, and once you start trying it, you may find that you can't stop.

It is my hope that I have played a part, by writing this story, to keep my grandmother's memory alive. As I said at the beginning, the hardest part of this endeavor has been to explain just what it was about Marn that made her so extraordinary. I dearly hope that my words have given you even the slightest glimpse of that.

Marn

Afterword

I remembered another Marnie story, and it seems fitting to add it here. She was reading a tough guy thriller paperback one time, seated in her special chair in her living room. She liked those Robert Ludlum-type stories. Anyway, at some point in this story, a character gets "blown away" by another character. Marn read this passage to me, and then sighed. "That's how I want to go, Kimmie," she said. "I want to blow away."

It is now more than three years since I set out to write Marn's story, and I am so glad I did. It has brought me more joy and pride and catharsis than I could have imagined. I'm grateful to have had such wonderful inspiration, the time to focus on it, and the patience of those around me. Also grateful am I for those who cheered me on as I posted the story in blog form. Your comments and messages bolstered me in the best way possible; you let me know I had a story that resonated with you.

Our Polly died a year ago last spring, the last of the Robinson gals to leave this earth. She also died young – younger even than Marn was when she passed – and just like each of them, Polly took a little bit of me with her when she went on her way.

I have this story to thank for getting as much time as I did with Polly at the end of her life. She was getting sick, and I stayed almost that whole last summer with her. I'd spend my day upstairs writing in a makeshift office I had created for myself, and then join her in the late afternoon out on the deck, where we'd sit together over a few vodkas and talk, watching the summer shadows grow long as darkness fell softly around us. She told me so many stories about all those who had gone before: Linda and Susan and Tom and Palmer, and of course Marn. She was very sad to be without them, especially her wonderful Palmer, and was unabashedly open about being ready to die. But she did love to talk about her family, and so did I, so we had a ball.

It was also during this time of writing that my own first grandchild was born, giving me a new connection to Marnie. Having had such a strong grandmother force in my childhood made me look so forward to becoming one myself. I could hardly wait, and it is everything I thought it would be. I only hope I can be half the grandmother the old gal was.

In closing, I thank my beautiful mom, and my aunts Susan and Polly, and especially my sweet little Marn, as though I were thanking my lucky stars. I will always treasure the memories of you, and I am proud and humbled to share you.

Providence, Rhode Island

Winter 2014

Made in the USA
Middletown, DE
22 November 2020

24773029R00083